Advance Praise for *Political Economy of Social Change and Development in Nepal*

Based on over 15 years of research, and drawing on all of the key studies of Nepali society and economy published over a similar period, Jeevan Sharma's book is a deeply insightful analysis of Nepal's complex transformation which transcends disciplinary boundaries. He describes a country which is now deeply penetrated by the ideas and material aspects of development, market and modernity, where all of the basic indicators of sustainable development have taken a sharp upward trend, but whose people face the 'stubborn continuities' of socioeconomic inequity and poor governance, obliging many of them to seek financial relief as migrant labourers on terms of unfreedom and precarity. Sharma offers us the most integrative, synoptic and interdisciplinary account of these changes and paradoxes published to date, and his book will, therefore, be an essential reading for anyone interested in modern and contemporary Nepal. Its critical use of Karl Polanyi's model of *The Great Transformation* will also be of great interest to readers concerned with the extent to which theoretical models developed in a Euro-American context are helpful for understanding social, political and economic transformations in the contemporary global South.

—Michael Hutt,
Emeritus Professor of Nepali and Himalayan Studies,
SOAS, University of London, UK

Jeevan Sharma has produced a stimulating and provocative 'monograph', as he calls it, on the political economy of social change and development in Nepal. Drawing on original field research and the ideas of Karl Polanyi on *The Great Transformation* as well as the secondary literature, Jeevan Sharma has produced an analysis that effectively challenges much of the conventional wisdom on, and provides a wholistic overview of, the political economy of development in Nepal over recent decades. It constitutes not only a synthesis of his own original research but also an ambitious attempt to provide an overall integrated theoretical framework for the broader analysis of political, social and economic change in Nepal over the recent decades.

His theoretical framework explicitly draws on Karl Polanyi's notion of 'great transformation', which he sees as involving both the emergence of a market economy and society and a countermovement of social protection in response to the negative effects of the capitalism—what Sharma refers to as 'a double movement'. But he also refers to more recent theorists, like Goodwin (2018) and Fraser (2013), and argues that what is needed is a framework that recognises the potential of a third 'countermovement', to fight inequality, hierarchy and domination—a movement of what Fraser calls 'emancipation'.

The framework espoused by Sharma is one that identifies a complex interaction between what might be termed economic, social and political movements or forces, which act in both complementary and contradictory ways to shape the 'great transformation' in any given part of the world. Even more than in the case of the initial 'great transformation' of Western Europe, the analysis of 'social change and development' in Africa, Asia and Latin America in the 20th and 21st century must also integrate the effects of the external forces of capitalism on a global scale.

Sharma seems to believe that, despite the momentous (step change) transformation of Nepal's economy, society and politics in recent decades, 'Nepal has not seen a countermovement from below', leaving the 'emancipation' of the Nepali people yet to be achieved. This seems to effectively consign the 10-year long Maoist insurgency or 'People's War' to the rubbish bin of history. For some, however, this will vindicate skepticism regarding the potential in the 21st century of armed struggle to achieve the kind of 'emancipation' to which Fraser refers. Readers may wish, in this regard, to revisit Eric

Wolf's great work, also based on a Polanyian perspective, *Peasant Wars of the Twentieth Century*, first published exactly 50 years ago. He included in his six case studies only those revolutions that were successful.

—David Seddon,
Former Professor at the School of Development Studies, University of East Anglia, UK

The causes and consequences of the mammoth changes that have roiled Nepali polity and society in the recent years have been a story waiting to be told, and that is what *Political Economy of Social Change and Development in Nepal* has managed to do. Unlike other impressionistic accounts, Jeevan Sharma marshals empirical facts he himself had gathered over the years in support of his argument. The result is this highly readable account of 'the great transformation', as he calls it, that has yet to come full circle but the outcome of which is there for all to see and understand through the eyes of a scholar grounded firmly in the reality of his home country.

—Deepak Thapa,
Director of Social Science Baha, Kathmandu, Nepal

Political Economy of Social Change and Development in Nepal

Political Economy of Social Change and Development in Nepal

Jeevan R. Sharma

B L O O M S B U R Y
NEW DELHI • LONDON • OXFORD • NEW YORK • SYDNEY

BLOOMSBURY INDIA
Bloomsbury Publishing India Pvt. Ltd
Second Floor, LSC Building No. 4, DDA Complex, Pocket C – 6 & 7,
Vasant Kunj New Delhi 110070

BLOOMSBURY, BLOOMSBURY ACADEMIC INDIA and the Diana logo are trademarks of Bloomsbury Publishing Plc

First published in India 2021
This edition published 2021

Bloomsbury Academic
An imprint of Bloomsbury Publishing Plc

ISBN: HB: 978-93-89449-22-8; eBook: 978-93-89449-24-2

2 4 6 8 10 9 7 5 3 1

Typeset in Minion pro by Manipal Technologies Limited
Printed and bound in India

Contents

Acknowledgements

This book is a synthesis of my research conducted over the last several years, in collaboration with colleagues, research partners and research participants in Nepal. Over the years, I have benefited from the inspiration, encouragement and generous support from many people in different places.

I am indebted to many people in and from Palpa, as well as other parts of Nepal, for their time, hospitality and insights that have enriched my research. My research in Nepal has benefitted from the assistance of Sanjay Aryal, Kiran Sharma, Sadixya Bista, Bijay Chettri, Ramakanta Tiwari and Samesh Adhikari—for which, I am very grateful.

Antonio Donini, with whom I carried out field research on social change in Nepal, has been a continuous source of encouragement and mentorship.

My work on the wider social, political and economic change in Nepal has benefitted from conversations with many people. In particular, I would like to acknowledge: Ian Harper, Roger Jeffery, Judith Justice, Radha Adhikari, Andrea Nightingale, David Seddon, Ben Campbell, Judith Justice, David Gellner, Avash Piya, Dyan Mazurana, Michael Hutt, Crispin Bates, Patricia Jeffery, Deepak Thapa, Qudsiya Contractor, Suryakant Waghmore, Bandita Sijapati, Sujeet Karn, Lynn Bennett, Norah Niland and Gael Robertson.

Chandra Sekhar at Bloomsbury believed in this project and has been extremely patient throughout. I would like to thank him, the three anonymous reviewers and editorial team at Bloomsbury, as well as the freelance copy editor, Catriona Child.

I would like to acknowledge my deep appreciation to friends and well-wishers in Nepal and around the world for their company, encouragement and stimulating insights.

Finally, my greatest thanks go to my family members in Nepal for their support. Aayona and Mona have been my greatest support for this book project, who have not only provided me with the time needed to complete this book, but have been patient with me when I could not be around. I started the book when we were expecting our son, Aahan, who is now 8 months old. I dedicate this book to him.

Jeevan R. Sharma
March 2021
Edinburgh

Small bazaars and towns are dominated by the signboards of remittance transfer companies, Palpa, 2008.

1

Introduction: Framing Nepal's Social Transformation

Nepal has been undergoing tumultuous sociopolitical and economic changes since the 1950s. At the macro level, politically, Nepal has leapfrogged from a feudal, hierarchical monarchy to a republican order that has attempted to engrain ideas of human rights, equality and inclusive citizenship. Economically, there has been a gradual shift in the political economy of rural livelihoods with the commodification of land and labour, the widespread flows of cash and financialisation and extensive outmigration, with the countryside deeply penetrated by the ideas as well as the material aspects of development, market and modernity. Nevertheless, amid these sea-changes is a story of stubborn continuities—the sustained inequalities, democracy drained by clientelist patterns of distribution and unrelenting poverty. The extractive model of development over the last seven decades has resulted in a huge regional disparity between the cosmopolitan capital city, Kathmandu, and relentless hardship in remote regions. Economic liberalisation since the late 1980s, which has been associated with marketisation and commodification of basic services, has had a significant impact on people's access to healthcare and education, and their ideas of rights and citizenship. More pertinently, the change itself has been remarkably uneven, where rapid changes in the nature of the political system and a new progressive constitutional order have not led to similar economic freedoms. In such a context, rural Nepali youth, both men and women, have continued to seek financial relief as migrant labourers in the far-flung economies of India, the Gulf and South East Asia, often on terms of unfreedom and precarious employment and despite reports of widespread exploitation and ill treatment (Thapa 2003, Sapkota 2016). The incorporation of the rural poor in the class-divided and racialised economies of the unequal geographies of the global labour market has profound consequences for the welfare and care of those left behind.

How might we account for these transformations and paradoxes? Scholarship on Nepal's culture, politics and economy has been fractured, shaped by disciplinary boundaries and prevailing theoretical priorities and perspectives. Historically, dominant scholarships have overwhelmingly focused on its stereotypical image as an underdeveloped, poor, agrarian, exotic country—characterised by hierarchies associated with Hindu religion, caste, gender and ethnicity. Not only has Nepal long been romanticised in Western eyes as an untouched 'Himalayan Shangri-La' and peasant society, but its interaction with wider global processes has been largely ignored or treated as secondary or considered exceptional. Overall, despite a strong tendency in the scholarship to view Nepali society as 'fatalist', bounded, immobile and sedentary within the Hindu framework of dharma and karma, ethnographic evidence shows remarkable connections, transformations, pragmatism and pluralism in people's worldviews and livelihoods. More specifically, what does it mean to talk about change, transformation and transition in Nepal beyond its stereotypical image of fatalism and immobility? How are powerful historical processes experienced and negotiated in Nepal? Not only have these transformations been uneven while creating new forms of consciousness and opportunities for earning cash to meet immediate needs, but they also produce new forms of precarity, citizenship claims and unaddressed grievances. How might we assess the paradoxical effects of these transformations in people's lives and livelihoods, both in terms of expanding ideas of rights and freedom, while also producing vulnerabilities and precarity?

Drawing on insights from field research carried out in Nepal since 2004, this book engages with these questions, and considers whether and how Nepal's political economy might have been transformed since the 1950s, while situating these changes in Nepal's modern history and its location in the global economic system. First, the book assembles and builds on the scholarship on Nepal from a multidisciplinary and synoptic perspective. In doing so, there is an attempt to go beyond the sedentary, immobile, fatalist and romanticised narrative of Nepal that has remained dominant in the orientalist scholarship on the country. Second, focusing on local discourses, experiences and expectations of transformations, the book draws our attention to how powerful historical processes are experienced and negotiated in Nepal, and assess how these may, at the same time, produce ideas of equality, human rights and citizenship, while also generating new forms of precarity. In particular, the book has been organised under four important transformations in Nepal's political economy since the 1950s:

1. A fundamental shift in the nature of the Nepali state from a deeply feudal and hierarchical society to one where the ideas of human rights and citizenship are pervasive;
2. Widespread commodification and global mobility of labour, impacting agricultural and land-based livelihoods and social relations;
3. The impact of widespread mobility of young women and men from rural Nepal, with diverse caste and ethnic backgrounds, as they seek to navigate and realise their educational, occupational and political aspirations, and struggle to overcome challenges in the process of mobility to the city;
4. Ideological, material and political consequences of aid-funded development projects and activities.

While all these themes have received attention from scholars, this book's overall aim is to offer a more integrative, synoptic and interdisciplinary account of these changes and paradoxes as a whole, under a single framework of 'great transformation'.[1] The book explains

1 I define and offer a discussion of the concept of 'great transformation' later in this chapter.

the nature and form of these transformations, explains their historical processes and limitations and indicates their consequences for lives and livelihoods. The style is designed to narrate these transformations and paradoxes in a way that makes the discussion relevant and accessible to non-specialist readers while framing them within a broader conceptual framework.

Nepal's Development Paradox

Since the 1950s, Nepal's political system has transitioned from the toppling of the 104-year-extractive-old Rana oligarchy to a decade of fragile experiment with democracy (1950–1960), succeeded by a 30-year-old absolute monarchy or the panchayat system (1960–1990); a re-ushering of multiparty democracy in 1990; a relapse into civil conflict in 1996 and a period of authoritarianism between 2002 and 2005. More recently, in 2006, Nepal emerged from a violent Maoist insurgency (1996–2005) and other identity-based social and political movements, most notably Adivasi Janajati,[2] Tharu[3] and Madhesi[4] movements, which were built around an agenda, which at their core attacked the feudal and exclusionary nature of Nepali society and its inherent structural inequalities. Since then, Nepal has witnessed a protracted and fraught political transition from a monarchical Hindu state to a secular democratic federal republic state, institutionalised in the form of a contested constitutional settlement that was promulgated in September 2015, following the devastating earthquake of April 2015, which simultaneously led to widespread violence in Nepal's Terai.

---

2 Non-Hindu ethnic groups or 'indigenous nationalities' with their own languages, cultures and history (*See*, Gellner 1997, Onta 2006, Toffin 2009, Hagen 2010).

3 Indigenous population living in certain regions of southern Nepal (*See*, Guneratne 1998, Fujikura 2007).

4 The Madhesis, who reside in the southern plains in Nepal, share deep cultural ties with people in Northern India, speak a variety of non-Nepali languages. Madhesis have been marginalised on the grounds of race, religion, language and citizenship (*See*, Gautam, 2008, Mathema 2011, Jha 2014).

The panchayat regime, grounded in the 'one nation–one culture' doctrine and in a centralised model of development, shaped contours to an exclusive state, which privileged the Hindu, upper-caste groups from the hills, marginalising the Janajatis, Dalits, rural peasants, women, as well as Madhesis, residing in the southern plains across the Indian border (Onta 1996, Pfaff-Czarnecka 1997). Similarly, the turn to democracy since 1990, with its unstable political coalitions and patronage politics, has significantly shaped distributional coalitions, facilitated by the increased allocation of budget in health, education, agriculture, road construction and other development projects and associated resource flows at local and national levels (Pfaff-Czarnecka 2008).

The tumultuous shifts have enabled the Nepali political economy to graduate from a deeply feudal and hierarchical society to one where the ideas of human rights and citizenship are pervasive. Mobilisations based on ethnicity, language, caste, gender and regional identities calling for recognition of historical and institutional exclusion and demanding institutional recognition, representation and redistribution of resources have been widespread. Pointed questions on the systematic marginalisation of Dalits, Adivasi Janajati, Tharu, women, third gender, Madhesis, people with disabilities and other subaltern groups have been raised, demanding rights, recognition, representation and redistribution of resources, including reservations system (Simkhada 2017, Sunam 2018). Exclusionary and extractive history has been fiercely challenged as never before through various social and political mobilisations ushering in new forms of consciousness.

These compressed tectonic sociopolitical shifts have been concurrently accompanied by economic shifts evident in the nature of livelihoods and intensification of development processes. Although Nepal continues to be viewed as an agrarian and peasant society, which is particularly evident in the discourses of the influential multilateral and bilateral development institutions, such as the

World Bank, United States Agency for International Development (USAID) and Department for International Development (DFID), along with Nepal's own policies and plans, livelihoods in once-remote regions are divorced from agriculture and land. Although subsistence agriculture remains a core feature of Nepal's representation in development discourses and planning processes, it does not produce viable income (Sharma 2008). While people do continue to identify themselves as farmers (*kisan*), it does not mean that agriculture is the mainstay of their livelihoods; instead, people must combine farming with other non-farm sources of income (Adhikari 2001, Mishra 2010, Sunam and McCarthy 2016). Over the years, the organisation of local labour and old production logics, primarily shaped by caste and ethnicity, have been largely replaced by commodified labour arrangements. The adoption of market economy principles and commodification of land and labour has been increasingly impacted by overseas labour migration that has intensified since the 1980s (Sunam and McCarthy 2016, Campbell 2018). Although Nepal has a long history of migration including the recruitment of Nepali men in British and Indian armies in the 19th century followed by different waves of outmigration (Sharma 2019, Subedi 2016, Gellner 2013, Seddon et al. 2001), widespread mobility and migration of young people from different caste and ethnic groups for work and education in the recent decades, both internally and externally, has reconfigured intergenerational contract, household livelihoods and caring arrangements, youth futures and social mobility. Not just big cities, but the landscape in the bazaars in the countryside, with steep increase in the price of land for building concrete houses and shops full of imported consumer goods and constant transaction of mobile recharge cards, are dominated by the signboards of remittance transfer companies, banks and other financial institutions, indicating profound finalisation of the rural economy.

Likewise, different development projects, many funded by foreign aid, have proliferated since the 1950s, heralding significant material, institutional and ideological consequences. Construction of roads and associated connectivity have led to widespread mobility of vehicles, goods and travellers that have reconfigured consumption, production and access to the market. The last seven decades have seen a large part of the development budget spent constructing roads connecting remote villages to market towns, cities and highways (Rankin et. al. 2017). Various reports indicate that cement consumption has increased at an annual rate of 10 per cent in the last decade. Reports have indicated unplanned road construction and the widespread importance and use of heavy equipment, such as backhoe loaders, excavators and diesel-hydraulic earthmovers, which have far-reaching environmental consequences for the region and beyond (Coburn 2020). There has been a surge in the consumption of imported goods, ranging from varieties of packaged food and drinks, concrete, mobile phones, television and a range of consumer goods, as well as access to credit from various banking and financial infrastructures in remote regions. According to the Demographic and Health Survey (DHS) of 2016, nearly 75 per cent women and 89 per cent of men own a mobile phone, and 41 per cent of women and 40 per cent of men use a bank account (The Ministry of Health or MoH, New Era and ICF 2017). According to reports, as of 2019, there are about 10 million Facebook users in Nepal. The widespread reach of mobile phone and social media have connected once-remote areas to the circulation of global and national cultural, political and economic spaces.

Health and educational infrastructures, public and (increasingly) private, have expanded to the once-remote areas. A report prepared by USAID, Nepal's key development partner since 1950, states, 'In 1951, only 1 per cent of the primary school-aged population was in primary school; the average Nepali could only expect to live 28 years, more than one-quarter of all Nepalis would die before their first birthday, literacy was only 2 per cent, the country had 300 college graduates' (Skerry et al. 1991: 370). By 2018, the literacy rate for 15–24 years had increased to 92.39 per cent, net primary school enrolment to

96 per cent and life expectancy to 70 years (UNESCO 2019). Similar advances are evident in the health sector. Over the last three decades, women's chances of survival during childbirth have greatly improved. Accordingly, Nepal has been hailed as a global success in reducing maternal mortality, because significant progress was made despite widespread poverty and a decade-long civil war. Demographic and Health Survey data show that the Maternal Mortality Ratio (MMR) decreased from 539 in 1996 to 239 in 2016 (MoH, New Era and ICF 2017). The push for institutional delivery and skilled birth attendants meant that more than half of the births (57 per cent) took place in health facilities in 2016 compared to only 8 per cent in 1996 in Nepal. Skilled assistance during childbirth has increased from 9 per cent in 1996 to 58 per cent in 2016 (MoH, New Era and ICF 2017). Despite this, poor maternal and child health remain key concerns in Nepal, as indicated in the widespread prevalence of home birth and lack of skilled birth attendants, especially for the poor. DHS data show high levels of disparity in terms of educational status, that is, 85 per cent of births to women with at least a School Leaving Certificate (SLC) were delivered in a health facility, compared with only 36 per cent of births to women with no education. Births to women in the highest wealth quintile were more likely (90 per cent) to occur at a health facility than births to women in the lowest quintile (34 per cent).

Major demographic shifts have occurred due to a transition from a high-mortality, high-fertility society to a low-mortality, low-fertility society within a relatively short period, with significant ramifications for gender, generation and the economy. Since 1980, Nepal saw significant declines in its total fertility rate, crude death rates and population growth, alongside significant improvements in life expectancy. The fertility rate, which measures the average number of children per couple, has been going down, from 6.68 in 1977 to 2.3 in 2016 (MoH, New Era and ICF 2017). A USAID report put the infant mortality rate (IMR) for 1952 at 255 per 1,000 (Skerry et al. 1991: 370). Most recent data put the neonatal mortality rate (NMR) at 21 per 1,000 live births and under-five mortality at 39 deaths per 1,000 live births (MoH, New Era and ICF 2017). Crude death rates in Nepal have decreased from 16.9 deaths per 1,000 in 1980–1985 to 6.5 in 2010–15. In 1980–1985, life expectancy at birth was 48.34 years, and it had increased to 69.01 years by 2010–2015. In 1980–1985, the average annual rate of population growth was 2.31 per cent. By 2005–2010, this growth rate had declined to 1.05 per cent per year.

Beyond these measurable impacts, maternal and child health and family planning programmes have significantly affected ideas about family, pregnancy, childbearing and child-rearing that had previously remained mostly unexplored (Brunson 2016).

Various community development programmes and social mobilisations and user and self-help groups in the fields of literacy, saving and credit, women's empowerment, agriculture, irrigation and forestry sectors have ushered a new era of deliberative grassroots democracy. It is estimated that there more than 400,000 community-based groups, operating as user groups or committees, throughout Nepal.[5] Complementing grassroots initiatives is the massive proliferation of NGOs, who have multiplied from 193 to 33,000 between 1990 and 2006 (Shah 2008). Many of these NGOs work towards delivering essential services, complementing the role of the state and the market. Other NGOs are more political in the sense that they work to improve the position of their members or constituency by raising their claims and rights. Working across the health, education, social welfare and development sectors, NGOs have spread ideas of human rights, equality and justice, thus, enlightening ordinary Nepalis about global narratives, resources and institutions.

Nevertheless, all these impressive changes have not altered the obstinate continuities of inequalities, discrimination and unrelenting poverty that have historically defined the Nepali state. Instead, by

5 https://publications.parliament.uk/pa/cm200910/cmselect/cmintdev/memo/nepal/ucm502.htm (accessed on 16 February 2021).

design or default, the consequences of these changes have exacerbated these continuities and unleashed a developmental paradox. Persistent horizontal inequalities have disproportionately affected the life chances of women, marginalised caste and ethnic groups and the poor (DFID and World Bank 2006). Human rights organisations consistently report that the poor and marginalised, most notably the Dalits, Madhesis and women, continue to be subjected to widespread violence and ill treatment. Protection from violence remains patchy. Despite the surge in development expenditure, the state has a poor record in providing basic services (Upreti et al. 2012). Human development reports have consistently reported significant disparities between regions.

While Nepali elections continue to attract an impressive number of voters and public debate on politics remains impressive, patronage continues to shape politics and the distribution of public goods and services (Justice 1986, Pfaff-Czarnecka 2008, Joshi and Mason 2011, Sharrock 2013). People speak of the duty of the Nepali state to provide effective and efficient services to the citizens, although the state rarely provides such services in practice to anyone except for those with social and political connections. Local people enthusiastically engage in public debate on the state's poor delivery of basic services, although few believe that their voice will have any impact. While the ideas of participation and inclusion have ushered new waves of grassroots democracy, the actual practices are often shaped by local power dynamics and fictitious records of participation in documents and minutes. Governance has been characterised by patronage and clientelism, and conflicts of interest are endemic in politics, business, bureaucracy, media and civil society at both local and national levels (Upadhya 2020, Thapa 2017). Reports highlight how the very cost of campaigning deters women and marginalised groups with limited economic resources from contesting elections (Samuhik Abhiyan 2018). Such enfeebling of state institutions and governance mechanism is confirmed by the World Bank's governance ranking of Nepal in the bottom 20th percentile on the rule of law, government effectiveness and political stability or absence of violence out of more than 200 countries. Even more damning is the fact that Nepal is performing worse in 2016 than in 2006 on critical measures of governance, apart from the measure on the prevalence of violence (World Bank 2018). The statistics of such a downward trend are given a lease of life by a barrage of reports on relatable examples. For instance, in 2018, only a few months after Nepal celebrated the first local government elections in 20 years, reports emerged of the election of more than 300 construction company owners, who were awarding themselves construction contracts (Pokharel 2018). Sidestepping public deliberations and formal processes, pertinent political decisions are finalised by informal closed-door negotiations and elite bargains in the name of consensus (Jha 2014, Sharma 2019). The 2015 constitution of Nepal, which had been in the making since 2006, and symbolised the transition to 'Naya Nepal' (or new Nepal), came to force not through democratic deliberations at the Constitutional Assembly, but through an agreement between the leaders of four main political parties. The aggregation of poor governance, corruption and financial scandals exposing political leaders and parties at national and local levels has led to an erosion of public trust in governance and state institutions. A survey by The Asia Foundation and Interdisciplinary Analysts in 2010 concluded that the process of public procurement is largely seen as unfair, with the majority believing that a personal connection with either government officials (88 per cent) or political parties (87 per cent) are requisites to obtaining such contracts (The Asia Foundation 2010). Questions on procurement irregularities by the political class have been widely reported in the Nepali media and public debate (Thapa 2017).

Not only have development infrastructures had a colossal impact on the life chances, health, well-being, freedom and mobility of ordinary citizens, but also the rapid commodification and marketisation of health and education since the 1990s have profoundly shaped ideas of rights and citizenship. The Nepali state's under-investment in essential services, such as the poor state of government schools or health posts or hospitals, co-exist with the expansion of private schools and medical practices in a context where the state's regulatory capacity is limited and ordinary citizens do not have the capacity to monitor or demand the service provision.

Unemployment and lack of jobs have meant that more than 1,000 economically active men and women migrate from Nepal every day, in search of employment opportunities in different overseas destinations. While remittance from outmigration has been the lifeline of Nepal's economy, with reports indicating that one-fifth of the poverty reduction in Nepal between 1995 and 2004 can be attributed to higher levels of work-related migration and remittances sent home (Lokshin et al. 2010), despite the difficult years during the insurgency, the hidden social impact of this scale of migration has been sobering. As Nepali migrants attempt to escape the precarious circumstances back home, they go to work in exploitative conditions in overseas destinations, get trapped in debt and many return as dead or injured bodies. Various reports have indicated widespread ill treatment of migrant workers in overseas destinations such as the Gulf States and Southeast Asian countries, although very little systematic documentation of this exists. Various reports indicate that anywhere between three to five dead bodies of migrant workers arrive in Nepal's Kathmandu airport daily. According to data collated by Nepal's Foreign Employment Board, from 2008–2009 to 2014–2015, a total of 4,322 migrant workers died across 24 destination countries (International Labour Organisation or ILO 2016).

Change, Transformation and Development in Nepal

Change, transformation and development have been recurrent themes, not only in everyday conversations, political rhetoric and social movements, but also in Nepali public culture and literary writings since the 1950s (Hutt 1994b, Grandin 1994a, Grandin 1994b). In the quick survey below, I do not attempt to offer a summary or detailed analysis of the rich body of scholarship and debate dealing with various aspects of Nepal's political, social and economic changes. Given the vast amount of scholarship and literary writings on this theme, I omit specifics and deal with the terrain of scholarship on change in Nepal with broad brush strokes.

A useful brief overview of social and political change in Nepal can be found in a recently published article titled 'The Changing Face of Nepal' in *Current History* (Hutt 2020). Nepal's significant political events in 1950, 1990 and 2006 have attracted significant attention from scholars, who offer insights on the nature and dynamics of the political movements and changes following those events (Joshi and Rose 1966, Raeper and Hoftun 1992, Uprety 1992, Hutt 1994a, Whelpton 2005, Dixit 2009, Jha 2014, Sharma 2019). Not surprisingly, a substantial amount of scholarship has delved into the roots and dynamics of Nepal's Maoist insurgency, post-conflict transition and state formation (Thapa 2003, Hutt 2004, Lecomte-Tilouine 2013, Zharkevich 2019a, Rankin et al. 2018, Gellner et al. 2016, Toffin 2013, Adhikari 2014, Paudel 2016). The cavalcade of scholarly engagement on the Nepali state's transformation, identity politics and environments, following the Maoist conflict and peace process, has been covered in a review article titled 'Nepal's Ongoing Political Transformation: A Review of Post-2006 Literature on Conflict, the State, Identities, and Environments' in Modern Asian Studies (Shneiderman et al. 2016). Situated within the wider political and legal changes, the study of social and political movements on the assertion of rights on the grounds of linguistic, ethnic and Janajati rights has attracted by far the most attention since the 1990s (Gellner, et al. 1997, Onta 2006, Gellner and Hachhethu 2008, Gellner 2009, Lecomte-Tilouine 2009, Hangen 2010, Lawoti and Hangen 2013, Adhikari and Gellner 2016). While the dominant discourses, sociopolitical movements and scholarly attention have focused on the structural violence that has emanated from ethnicity in the recent years, unlike in neighbouring India, until recently, the situation of Nepali Dalits and their assertation has received limited attention in public debate (Folmar 2007, Vasily 2009, Aahuti 2010, B. K. 2013, Pariyar and Lovett 2016). Reflecting the rise of Madhesi political mobilisation, which since 2006 has been cardinal in shaping the debate and policies on state restructuring and federalism in Nepal, there has been a resurgence of interest in examining Madhesi politics, including the centrality of Madhesi movement in shaping the debate and political momentum for federalism in Nepal (Gautam 2008, Mathema 2011, Jha 2014). While there has been a strong tendency to view Nepali women as a homogeneous group, suffering mainly as a result of traditional Hindu religious and ritual practices (Bennett 1983), emergent studies have documented women's agency, dynamism, change and experiential differences (Sob 1997, Des Chene 1997, Adhikari 2019, Shah 2018, Yadav 2016, Ahearn 2004, Tamang 2002, Rai 2020). Scholars have offered an analysis of the impact of Nepal's Maoist insurgency on increased awareness and confidence, respect for and greater political representation of women in Nepal (Manchanda 2004, Leve 2007, Yadav 2016). Attention has also been paid to the changing situation of the labouring population, including bonded labourers, in the context of major political, legal and economic changes including insightful peasant histories from below (Holmberg and March 1999, Giri 2010, Raj 2010, Maycock 2018, Hoffmann 2018). To date, Nepali historian Mahesh Chandra Regmi's monographs remain the only major works on economic history that outlines the nature and change of land, labour and economic relations in 18th-, 19th- and 20th-century Nepal (Regmi 1961, Regmi 1976, Regmi 1978, Regmi 1988). In recent years, a few attempts have been made to document the impact of economic changes within the framework of market liberalisation (Rankin 2004, Shakya 2013, Shakya 2018, Mahat 2020), including in the context of Nepal's post-earthquake reconstruction (Paudel et. al. 2020, Le Billon et. al. 2020, Hutt et al. 2021). In addition, some scholars have been focusing on rural agrarian change and political economy in the context of Nepal's incorporation into global capital (Blaikie et al. 1980, Adhikari 2001, Sugden 2013, Sunam and McCarthy 2016) and the gendered and sociocultural consequences of these changes (Sharma 2019, Campbell 2018, Zharkevich 2019b).

Overall, macro-political changes and the emergence of social and political movements on the assertation of different forms of identities have received significant scholarly attention in the last two to three decades. These studies have offered empirical and analytical insights on the rise and nature of the politics of ethnicity and the rise of new claims of citizenship in Nepal. Partly shaped by disciplinary boundaries and methodological framings, insightful studies on political economy, rural livelihoods and Nepal's incorporation in the global economy have not been in conversation with scholarship on the assertion of identities, human rights and citizenship or vice versa. Except in a few cases, the nature and consequences of political and economic forces, such as development activities or migration, beyond the boundary of the nation-state, have been largely overlooked. Existing scholarship and debates have offered important insights into different aspects of political, social and economic changes, but they do not offer a synoptic and integrative understanding of transformations and how different themes are intertwined. In a series of commentaries published in Nepali magazines, Chaitanya Mishra has alerted that Nepal's impressive political transition is not just a result of immediate social and political movements but is rooted in the structural transformation in livelihoods and changes in family and kinship structures associated with out-migration, non-farm economy, education amongst others (Mishra 2010). Moreover, the existing scholarship does not help us understand how impressive political transformations, the assertion of rights, rapid political-economic changes in rural livelihoods and new forms of precarity produced by market forces are related. We lack a single integrated framework that encompasses different dimensions of these transformations.

Overall, scholarship on change tends to focus on a single aspect, usually political or a recent surge in identity politics, which is not integrated with other aspects of change. For the most part, political scientists or political anthropologists isolate political change and identity politics from economic change, while most critics of political economy fail to consider that domain in relation to the recent call for human rights and citizenship and identity politics. Moreover, neither camp has paid much attention to social reproduction linked to transnational forces. In the context of intense political, economic and social transformation, we need a framework that encompasses different dimensions of change and explores how they are intertwined.

A Framework for Studying Social Change and Development

In this book, I use the concept of 'great transformation' as a promising integrative framework to make sense of the qualitative political, social and economic changes taking place in Nepal since 1950. I do so while acknowledging the historical legacies shaping these changes since 1950, as well as considering the political and economic forces that emanate from forces outside Nepal's political boundary. I use the concept of great transformation in two ways. First, I describe the irreversible qualitative 'step-change' in the way politics, economy and society are organised, that is, beyond the continual or 'normal' processes of incremental change (Castles 2001), noting that such transformation is fraught with tensions and paradoxes. All the empirical examples I use in this book attest to these transformations, which are organised under the four chapters. Secondly, I also talk about 'great transformation' in more specific analytical terms, as explained by Karl Polanyi. Below, let me briefly explain Polanyi's concept of the Great Transformation.

In his popular book, *The Great Transformation: The Political and Economic Origins of Our Times* (1944), Karl Polanyi developed the idea of *double movement* in Europe in the 19th and 20th centuries (Polanyi 1944/2001). The first was the movement from the pre-market and pre-industrial system when economic activity was rooted in familial, kinship, religious or political obligations and regulations, which Polanyi called *the market society* of the 19th century. The second was a countermovement to the first, that is, when the disruptive impact of *market society* led to poverty, unemployment, ecological crisis and insecurity of livelihoods, this was brought under control through state regulation, reform and social protection policies (Dale 2010, Goodwin 2018).

For Polanyi, the commodification of labour, land and money in Europe was a key historical moment in the creation of a market society. This socio-economic form of market society, which emerged in Britain in the 19th century, was fundamentally different from that of the past. Polanyi used the concept of 'embeddedness' to explain this historical transformation, and argued that, whereas the economy was previously embedded in social institutions and was subject to moral and ethical norms and political regulation, society, morals, ethics and politics were now embedded in the economy (Goodwin 2018, Fraser 2014). Thus, the market was given autonomy to operate according to its own logic, and society was required to adjust to market mechanisms.

In Polanyi's concept of market society, land, labour and money are called 'fictitious commodities' (Polanyi 1944/2001). He argued, land, labour and money perform multiple non-economic functions in society and, therefore, cannot be reduced to mere items of exchange or factors of production (Goodwin 2018). Polanyi argued that a truly self-regulating system of a price-making market was impossible, and thus claimed that the economy was not completely free of political and social influence. He used the concept of 'countermovement' to explain this political possibility, and argued that fictitious commodification of land, labour and money exposed societies to the logic of the market mechanism, which triggered 'countermovements' for the protection of society from the destructive influence of markets (Goodwin 2018). The overall feature of the great transformation was to protect people's lives from impersonal market forces, so that the market served society rather than society being subordinate to the market (Stewart 2006, Fraser 2014). In Polanyi's framework, the conflict between the proponents of the free market and social protection led to political stalemate and fascism (Polanyi 1994/2001).

In recent decades, there has been a growing trend to use Polanyi's concept of great transformation and *double movement* in the Global South. At this stage, it is useful to make a few clarificatory points on the usefulness of Polanyi's framework in contemporary Nepal. Polanyi's key concept of *double movement* focused on the nature and impact of the transformation of the market and attempts to protect society from the disruptive effects in the context of 19th and 20th century Britain. He did not write about developing countries like Nepal. For Polanyi, developing countries offered a case to compare and contrast with the development of capitalism in Europe (Stewart 2006). Of course, Nepal has had a very different economic and political history to western Europe, and we should not adopt Polanyi's framework uncritically. However, this contextual difference does not dismiss the importance of Polanyi's work, but rather points to the necessity of broadening its theoretical purview to better account for the specificities of contemporary transformation in developing countries like Nepal.

Reviewing the scholarship that uses Polanyi's double movement in the context of the Global South, Goodwin argues that it has mainly been employed to interrogate neoliberal capitalism. Accordingly, these studies fail to account for long-term processes of commodification and contestations in the Global South (Goodwin 2018). He calls for a more critical approach to double movement and great transformation and offers a framework to understand the development of the capitalism that emerged before structural adjustment and neoliberal reform in the Global South. The key implication of this call is to point towards the historical continuities of capitalist developments. Goodwin argues that capitalist development involves a simultaneous process of commodification and decommodification, rather than a linear process. Here, economic liberalisation is seen as a critical factor causing commodification and socio-economic dislocation, which invites countermovement in the form of social unrest and campaigns for social protection. Following pressure from beneath, the states introduce legal and social protection to protect people's livelihoods from the market fluctuations. Polanyi explicitly stated that the countermovement and pressure for social protection originated within society. For Polanyi, the state is seen as the vehicle through which the countermovement channelled its demands (Goodwin 2018). Calling this framing of Polanyi's work a 'soft' reading of double movement, Goodwin (2018) argues that Polanyi depicted a relatively simple, unidirectional political process, in which social pressure was converted into laws and policies through representative democratic institutions (Goodwin 2018, 1272–1273). The Great Transformation does not have room for the nature of state and patronage politics, complex bureaucratic practices and failure, on the part of the intellectual class to raise the questions of subsistence that characterise developing countries like Nepal. The nature of the state and patronage that benefit the ruling coalitions are overlooked. The limits of representative democracies, contested state-society, the role of civil society and the complexity of the political and bureaucratic process behind the design and implementation of laws and policies are completely absent from Polanyi's analysis (Goodwin 2018).

Nancy Fraser argues that Polanyi's work offers promising basis for analysis of structural transformation in the contemporary world. Despite the apparent widespread commodification, we lack progressive and institutionalised social movements to counter commodification and protect society from the whims of market (Fraser 2013). Fraser suggests that usual explanations for absence of social movements, such as the lack of leadership, the nature of precarious and fragmented labour or the nation-state framing, are inadequate. Instead, she urges to pay attention to social movements that do not find any place within the scheme of Polanyian double movement. The aim of these social movements is to fight domination that emanate from within society and not protect society from the destructive impact of market. In fact, these movements focused on a cultural critique of domination, hierarchies and social exclusions (Fraser 2014).

'What Polanyi failed to note was that the construction of "labour power" as a fictitious commodity rested on the simultaneous co-construction of "care" as a non-commodity. The unwaged labour of social reproduction supplied wage labour's necessary conditions of possibility; the latter could not exist, after all, in the absence of housework, child-raising, schooling, affective care and a host of other activities that maintain social bonds and shared understandings' (Fraser 2014, 550). Polanyi's work focused exclusively on the harms originating in the 'self-regulating market', and, thus, overlooks injustices emanating from within society, such as caste, ethnic exclusion, patriarchy and slavery, which depend on social constructions of labour, land and money, as non-commodities precisely (Fraser 2014).

Given such a situation, Fraser sees the third political project emerging from these social movements, which she calls emancipation. Accordingly, instead of *double movement*, Fraser suggests a framework of *triple movement*, that is, a three-sided constellation of conflict among proponents of marketisation, adherents of social protection and partisans of emancipation. In this way, Polanyi's framework connects politics, economy and social reproduction (Fraser 2014). Here, in theory, we have a situation where, while social protection offers relief from destructive forces of markets upon communities, it does not challenge domination in society. Similarly, marketisation may have destructive effects on society as Polanyi argued, but it can also have empowering effects when it destroys domination in society. Likewise, emancipation may not only bring freedom, but also weaken the fabric of solidarities and ethical basis of social protection, thereby, clearing paths for marketisation (Fraser 2013). Fraser points to a dangerous situation, where the neoliberal party adopts the vocabulary of emancipation and rights to weaken the socially protected as a champion on freedom, while proponents of social protection find themselves exposed by the critique of domination.

Therefore, in this book, as I have indicated above, instead of limiting the analysis only to the transformation of the market from the pre-market to the market society, and the countermovement, which is the core focus of Polanyian analysis, I extend Polanyi's framework of great transformation to offer an integrative account of changes in Nepal's politics, society and economy. In Nepal, alongside changes in the nature of the market economy and livelihoods, substantial shifts have occurred in political domains with highly contentious identity politics and struggles for recognition that have significantly impacted people's subjectivities and consciousness.

Thus, while the concept of countermovement offers a useful framework to explore struggles linked to rights and protection, it must be contextualised to capture the complexity of these processes in developing countries like Nepal. It also begs a simple question: what if political changes and discourses of equality, rights and citizenship are not accompanied by countermovements for economic freedoms and social protection? Or, what if a countermovement to challenge commodification simply fails to emerge?

Methods and Fieldwork

This monograph draws on materials and insights from my research in Nepal over the last 15 years. In 2004–2005, I conducted a year-long ethnographic fieldwork in a village inhabited by Bahun, Magar and

Dalits in Palpa district as a part of my doctoral research on male labour migrants, who travelled to India for work (Sharma 2019). As a part of this research, I also followed young men who travelled to Mumbai, Tansen and Kathmandu for work. While the primary focus of my initial fieldwork was on the gendered culture of migration (Sharma 2019), the fieldwork in the region gave insights on the changing village life, agrarian relations, including the Maoist insurgency, caste relations, gender dynamics and the expansion of roads and markets.

Primarily, this book is inspired by the fieldwork I conducted in Palpa in 2004–2005 and several follow-up field visits I have made to the region since. It also builds on insights gained from subsequent fieldwork conducted in other districts of Nepal (Dang, Rolpa, Doti, Kailali, Rupandehi, Morang and Dadeldhura) as a part of a research programme on 'Maoist conflict, aid, migration and social transformation' based at Tufts University.[6] Between 2007 and 2009, I returned to my original fieldwork village in Palpa, and to several other districts (Morang, Rupandehi, Dang, Rupandehi, Kailali, Doti and Dadeldhura), to conduct interviews with informants on the Maoist insurgency and local perceptions of social transformation (Sharma and Donini 2010). During this fieldwork, I also interviewed young men and women in Banglung, Palpa, Dang and Rolpa, who had joined the Maoist movement as combatants and activists. As a follow-up, in 2011, with the help of a few field assistants, I conducted research on the nature of changes in labour relations and mobility in western Nepal (Sharma and Donini 2012). In 2012 and 2013, I conducted fieldwork looking at the experiences of internal migrants within Nepal, particularly those employed in brick kilns, domestic work and construction work, as well as those who travelled across the border to India (Donini et al. 2013).

6 I acknowledge the fieldwork I conducted with my colleague Antonio Donini at Tufts University in various parts of Nepal between 2008 and 2013.

Conducted during the period of Nepal's post-conflict political transition, this fieldwork offered insights on local discourses, perceptions and expectations on the discourses of social change. In particular, the fieldwork did not just focus on local discourses on social change in the context of Nepal's recent political transition, but also on Nepal's incorporation into the global, political and economic flows, with a particular focus on development and migration.

Arguments and Organisation of the Monograph

One of the first arguments of the book is that alongside Nepal's dramatic political transition, there is clear evidence of a qualitative 'step-change' in the way Nepali society and economy are organised, which is beyond the 'normal' processes of incremental change. However, these social transformations have not been linear from unfreedom to freedom or subjects to citizens, but are characterised by fault lines and new forms of precarity. There is an apparent paradox in the nature of social transformation in Nepal. On the one hand, alongside significant political transformation, there has been recognition of historical inequalities and calls for rights and citizenship led by potent social and political movements. Likewise, land-based and caste-based social inequalities have been weakened if not completely dismantled, with increased opportunities for outmigration and cash flow from remittances. On the other hand, Nepal's incorporation into the global market, primarily through the extraction of its labour force and development processes, has produced new forms of suffering and precarity. Widespread consciousness of historical marginalisation and calls for rights and citizenship, together with increased opportunities for labour outmigration, have certainly offered aspirations and ideas of freedom for the historically marginalised and labouring population, away from old forms of precarity rooted in caste-attached labour and feudal production logics. Yet, the actual experiences of labour outmigration are exposing the migrants and their households to new forms of risks and precarity. Despite this, Nepal has not seen a 'countermovement from below' in the Polanyian sense, to articulate and address the adverse consequences of recent political-economic configurations associated with labour migration or extractive development processes. Development activities have opened up space for market penetration and deepening patronage, and old vulnerabilities of land and caste-based production systems have been replaced by new forms of precarity, dislocations and suffering. Thus, while there have been tectonic shifts in Nepal's politics, society and economy, great transformation in the strict Polanyian sense is unlikely in Nepal, where the movement from below to tackle social protection concerns is simply not there. In addition, well-articulated discourses of rights, equality and citizenship in the country have rarely included questions of livelihoods or subsistence aimed at material improvements of the marginalised and poor.

The remainder of this book follows the arguments indicated below:

Chapter Two focuses on Nepal's transformation from a profoundly feudal and hierarchical society to one where ideas of rights and citizenship are pervasive. This chapter outlines a major sociopolitical change underway in Nepali society in terms of citizenship, which broadly corresponds to the Nepali state's political transformation from an absolute monarchy to a constitutional monarchy and, then, to a republican state. This chapter looks at how the combination (and, sometimes, the competition) of social and political mobilisations under the guises of Maoist insurgency and ethnic and regional social movements, in parallel with the development of formal and non-formal education, community organisation and opening up of the rural areas to the market and public sphere(s), has resulted in a historical transformation of consciousness. Awareness of rights and gender has increased massively; the collective agency of women and oppressed and marginalised groups has escalated and resulted in durable changes in how individuals, groups and institutions interrelate.

Chapter Three focuses on the transformation of rural livelihoods from land and agriculture to non-land and non-agricultural sources, and the associated process of commodification and global mobility of labour. Rooted in Nepal's history and culture, migration and mobility have significantly shaped the political economy of rural livelihoods, bringing new opportunities to meet the needs of cash and social mobility. However, overseas labour migration has also brought new forms of insecurities and precarities.

Chapter Four focuses on the educational, occupational and political aspirations of young women and men from rural Nepal, with diverse caste and ethnic backgrounds, in the process of moving to the city. Focusing on the educational and employment strategies of young people from rural areas, it shows how young people may be leading a major social change from below in Nepal.

Chapter Five reflects on Nepal's history and politics of planned development from the vantage point of power, patronage and politics. Focusing on the real politics of development, it focuses on how things get done, rather than how things ought to be done. Moreover, it examines how ideas of development have, in fact, not only created new citizens, but have also created vulnerabilities through distributional coalitions that are firmly rooted in clientelism and patronage politics in Nepal.

Chapter Six concludes with the argument that social transformation has generated new forms of livelihood risks visible in terms of a development paradox with no social protection. It highlights practical implications for the distribution of social and economic protection of poor populations.

References

Aahuti. 2010. *Nepalma Varnavyavastha ra Barga-Sangharsha*. Lalitpur: Samata Foundation.

Adhikari, A. 2014. *The Bullet and the Ballot Box*. London and New York: Verso Books.

Adhikari, J. 2001. 'Mobility and Agrarian Change in Central Nepal'. *Contributions to Nepalese Studies*, 28: 247–267.

Adhikari, K.P. and D.N. Gellner. 2016. 'New Identity Politics and the 2012 Collapse of Nepal's Constituent Assembly: When the Dominant Becomes "Other"'. *Modern Asian Studies*, 50(6): 2009–2040.

Adhikari, R. 2019. *Migrant Health Professionals and the Global Labour Market: The Dreams and Traps of Nepali Nurses*. Oxford and New York: Routledge.

Ahearn, L.M. 2004. *Invitation to Love: Literacy, Love Letters and Social Change in Nepal*. New Delhi: Adarsh Books.

Bennett, L. 1983. *Dangerous Wives and Sacred Sisters: Social and Symbolic Roles of High Caste Women in Nepal*. Columbia University Press: New York.

BK, A.B. 2013. 'The Stigma of the Name: Making and Remaking of Dalit Identity in Nepal'. *Baha Occasional Papers 6*. Kathmandu: Himal Books.

Blaikie, P., J. Cameron, and D. Seddon. 1980. *Nepal in Crisis: Growth and Stagnation at the Periphery*. Delhi: Oxford University Press.

Brunson, J. 2016. *Planning Families in Nepal: Global and Local Projects of Reproduction*. New Brunswick: Rutgers University Press.

Campbell, B. 2018. 'Moral Ecologies of Subsistence and Labour in a Migration Affected Community of Nepal'. *Journal of the Royal Anthropological Institute*, 24 (S1): 151–165.

Castles, S. 2001. 'Studying Social Transformation'. *International Political Science Review*, 22(1): 13–32.

Coburn, B. 2020. *Nepal's Road-Building Spree Pushes into the Heart of the Himalayas*. Yale Environment 360. Available at: https://e360.yale.edu/features/paving-the-himalayas-a-road-building-spree-rolls-over-nepal (Accessed on 10 February 2021).

Dale, G. 2010. *Karl Polanyi: The Limits of the Market*. Cambridge: Polity Press.

Des Chene, M. 1997. 'Nepali Women's Movement: Experiences, Critiques, Commentaries'. *Studies in Nepali History and Society* 2(2): 291–297.

Dixit, K.M. 2009. *Dekheko Muluk*. Lalitpur: Jagadamba Prakashan.

DFID/World Bank. 2006. *Unequal Citizens: Gender, Caste and Ethnic Exclusion in Nepal*. Kathmandu: DFID/World Bank.

Donini, A., J.R. Sharma, and S. Aryal. 2013. *Structural Violence and Social Suffering among Marginal Nepali Migrants*. Medford, MA: Feinstein International Center, Tufts University.

Fraser, N. 2013. 'A Triple Movement? Parsing the Politics of Crisis after Polanyi'. *New Left Review*, 81: 119–132.

Fraser, N. 2014. 'Can Society Be Commodities All the Way Down? Post-Polanyian Reflections on Capitalist Crisis'. *Economy and Society*, 43(4): 541–558.

Folmar, S. 2007. 'Identity Politics among Dalits in Nepal'. *Himalaya*, 27(1): 41–53.

Fujikura, T. 2007. 'The Bonded Agricultural Labourers' Freedom Movement in Western Nepal'. In *Political and Social Transformations in North India and Nepal*, edited by H. Ishii, D. Gellner, and K. Nawa, 2: 319–359. New Delhi: Manohar Books.

Gautam, B., ed. 2008. *Madhes Bidrohako Nalibeli*. Kathmandu, Nepal: Martin Chautari.

Gellner, D.N., ed. 2009. *Ethnic Activism and Civil Society in South Asia*. New Delhi: Sage.

Gellner, D.N. 2013. 'Warriors, Workers, Traders, and Peasants: The Nepali/Gorkhali Diaspora since the Nineteenth Century'. In *Routledge Handbook of South Asian Diasporas*, edited by D. Washbrook and J. Chatterjee, 136–150. Abingdon and New York: Routledge.

Gellner, D.N. and K. Hachethu, eds. 2008. *Local Democracy in South Asia: Microprocesses of Democratization in Nepal and Its Neighbours*. New Delhi: Sage.

Gellner, D.N., Pfaff-Czarnecka, and J. Whelpton, eds. 1997. *Nationalism and Ethnicity in a Hindu Kingdom*. Netherlands: Harwood Academic Publishers.

Gellner, D.N., S.L. Hausner, and C. Letizia, eds. 2016. *Religion, Secularism and Ethnicity in Contemporary Nepal*. Oxford University Press: Delhi.

Giri, B.R. 2010. 'Bonded Labour Practice in Nepal: The Promise of Education as a Magnet of Child Bondedness'. *South Asia Research*, 30(2):145–164.

Goodwin, G. 2018. 'Rethinking the Double Movement: Expanding the Frontiers of Polanyian Analysis in the Global South'. *Development and Change*, 49(5): 1268–1290.

Grandin, I. 1994a. '"To Change the Face of This Country": Nepalese Progressive Songs under Panchayat Democracy'. *Journal of South Asian Literature*, 29(1): 175–189.

Grandin, I. 1994b. 'Nepalese Urbanism: A Musical Exploration'. In *Anthropology of Nepal: People, Problems and Processes*, edited by Michael Allen, 160–175. Kathmandu: Mandala Book Point.

Guneratne, A. 1998. 'Modernization, the State, and the Construction of a Tharu Identity in Nepal'. *The Journal of Asian Studies*, 57(3): 749–773.

Hagen, S. L. 2010. *The Rise of Ethnic Politics in Nepal: Democracy in the Margins*. London: Routledge.

Hoffmann, M. 2018. *The Partial Revolution: Labour, Social Movements and the Invisible Hand of Mao in Western Nepal*. Oxford and New York: Berghahn Books.

Holmberg, D. and K. March. 1999. 'Local Production/Local knowledge: Forced Labour from Below'. *Studies in Nepali History and Society*, 4(1): 5–64.

Hutt, M., ed. 1994a. *Nepal in the Nineties: Versions of the Past, Visions of the Future*. Delhi: Oxford University Press.

Hutt, M. 1994b. 'The Nepali Literature of the Democracy Movement and Its Aftermath'. In *Nepal in the Nineties: Versions of the Past, Visions of the Future*, edited by Michael Hutt, 82–97. Delhi: Oxford University Press.

Hutt, M., ed. 2004. *Himalayan 'People's War': Nepal's Maoist Rebellion*. London: Hurst & Co.

Hutt, M. 2020. 'The Changing Face of Nepal'. *Current History*, 119 (816): 141–145.

ILO. 2016. *When the Safety of Nepali Migrant Workers Fails: A Review of Data on the Numbers and Causes of the Death of Nepali Migrant Workers*. Kathmandu: ILO.

Hutt, M., M. Liechty, and S. Lotter. 2021 (Forthcoming). *Epicentre to Aftermath: Rebuilding and Remembering in the Wake of Nepal's Earthquakes*. New Delhi: Cambridge University Press.

Jha, P. 2014. *Battles of the New Republic: A Contemporary History of Nepal*. London: C Hurst & Co.

Joshi, B.L. and L.E. Rose. 1966. *Democratic Innovations in Nepal: A Case Study of Political Acculturation*. Berkeley and Los Angeles: University of California Press.

Joshi, M. and T. Mason, T. 2011. 'Peasants, Patrons, and Parties: The Tension between Clientelism and Democracy in Nepal'. *International Studies Quarterly*, 55(1): 151–175.

Justice, J. 1986. *Policies, Plans and People: Foreign Aid and Health Development*. Berkeley: University of California Press.

Lawoti, M. and S. Hagen, eds. 2013. *Nationalism and Ethnic Conflict in Nepal: Identities and Mobilization after 1990*. London: Routledge.

Le Billon, M.S. Phillippe, J. Baniya, B. Limbu, D. Paudel, K. Rankin, N. Rawal, and S. Schneiderman. 2020. 'Disaster Financialization: Earthquakes, Cashflows, and Shifting Household Economies'. *Development and Change*, 51(4): 939–969.

Lecomte-Tilouine, M. 2009. *Hindu Kingship, Ethnic Revival and Maoist Rebellion in Nepal*. New Delhi: Oxford University Press.

Lecomte-Tilouine, M. 2013. *Revolution in Nepal: An Anthropological and Historical Approach to the People's War*. New Delhi: Oxford University Press.

Leve, L. 2007. '"Failed Development" and Rural Revolution in Nepal: Rethinking Subaltern Consciousness and Women's Empowerment'. *Anthropological Quarterly*, 80(1): 127–172.

Lokshin, M., M. Bontch-Osmolovski, and E. Glinskaya. 2010. 'Work-Related Migration and Poverty Reduction in Nepal'. *Review of Development Economics*, 14 (2): 323–332.

Mahat, R. S. 2020. *Trials, Tremors and Hope: The Political Economy of Contemporary Nepal*. New Delhi: Adroit Publishers.

Manchanda, R. 2004. 'Maoist Insurgency in Nepal: Radicalizing Gendered Narratives'. *Cultural Dynamics*, 16(2/3): 237–58.

Mathema, K.B. 2011. *Madheshi Uprising: The Resurgence of Ethnicity*. Kathmandu: Mandala Book Point.

Maycock, M. 2018. *Masculinity and Modern Slavery in Nepal: Transitions into Freedom*. London: Taylor and Francis.

Ministry of Health Nepal, New ERA, and ICF. 2017. *Nepal Demographic and Health Survey 2016*. Kathmandu, Nepal: Ministry of Health, Nepal.

Mishra, C. 2010. *Badalindo Nepali Samaj*. Kathmandu: Fine Prints.

Onta. P. 1996. 'Ambivalence Denied: The Making of Rastriya Itihas in Panchayat Era Textbooks'. *Contributions to Nepalese Studies*, 23(1): 213–54.

Onta, P. 2006. 'The Growth of the Adivasi Janjati Movement in Nepal after 1990: The Non-Political Institutional Agents'. *Studies in Nepali History and Society*, 11(2): 303–354.

Pariyar, B. and J. C. Lovett. 2016. 'Dalit Identity in Urban Pokhara, Nepal'. *Geoforum*, 75: 134–147.

Paudel, D. 2016. 'The Double Life of Development: Empowerment, USAID and the Maoist Uprising in Nepal'. *Development and Change*, 47(5): 1025–1050.

Paudel, D., K. Rankin, and P. Le Billon. 2020. 'Lucrative Disaster: Financialization, Accumulation and Post-earthquake Reconstruction in Nepal'. *Economic Geography*, 96(2): 137–160.

Pfaff-Czarnecka, J. 1997: 'Vestiges and Visions: Cultural Change in the Process of Nation-Building in Nepal'. In *Nationalism and Ethnicity in a Hindu Kingdom,* edited by D.N. Gellner et al., 419–470. Amsterdam: Harwood Academic Publishers.

Pfaff-Czarnecka, J. 2008. 'Distributional Coalitions in Nepal: An Essay on Democratization, Capture, and (lack of) Confidence'. In *Local Democracy in South Asia: Microprocesses of Democratization in Nepal and Its Neighbours*, edited by D.N. Gellner and K. Hachethu, 71–104. New Delhi: Sage.

Pokharel, M. 2018. *Elected Contractors, Himal Khabarpatrika*, February 2018. Available at: http://archive.nepalitimes.com/article/from-nepalipress/

Elected-contractors,4182 (Accessed on 10 February 2021).

Polanyi, K. 1944. *The Great Transformation*. Boston: Beacon Press.

Raeper, W. and Hoftun, M. 1992. *Spring Awakening: An Account of the 1990 Revolution in Nepal*. New Delhi and New York: Viking.

Rai, K. 2020. '"Nepali" versus "Nepalka Mahila": Mahila Aandolanharu ra Bididhata'. *Samaj Adhyayan*, 15: 9–32.

Raj, Y. 2010. *History as Mindscapes: A Memory of the Peasants' Movement of Nepal*. Kathmandu: Martin Chautari.

Rankin, K. 2004. *The Cultural Politics of Markets: Economic Liberalization and Social Change in Nepal*. London: Pluto Press.

Rankin, K., A. Nightingale, P. Hamal, and T. Sigdel. 2018. 'Roads of Change: Political Transition and State Formation in Nepal's Agrarian Districts'. *Journal of Peasant Studies*, 45(2), 280–299.

Rankin, K., T. Sigdel, L. Rai, S. Kunwar, and P. Hamal. 2017. 'Political Economics and Political Rationalities of Road Building in Nepal'. *Studies in Nepali History and Society*, 22(1): 43–84.

Regmi, M.C. 1961. 'Recent Land Reforms in Nepal'. *Asian Survey*, 1(7): 32–37.

Regmi, M.C. 1976. *Landownership in Nepal*. California: University of California Press.

Regmi, M.C. 1978. *Thatched Huts and Stucco Palaces: Peasants and Landlords in the 19th Century Nepal*. New Delhi: Vikas.

Regmi, M.C. 1988. *An Economic History of Nepal, 1846–1901*. Varanasi: Nath.

Samuhik, Abhikyan. 2018. *Following the Money Campaign Expense Monitoring During the House of Representatives Election, 2017*. Kathmandu: Samuhik Abhiyan. PDF available at: https://www.ifes.org/sites/default/files/following_the_money_2018_english.pdf (Accessed on 11 May 2021).

Sapkota, J.R. 2016. *Kahar Vaidesik Rojgarile Bitholido Samaj*. Kathmandu: We Read.

Seddon, D., J. Adhikari, and G. Gurung. 2001. *The New Lahures: Foreign Employment and Remittance Economy of Nepal*. Kathmandu: NIDS.

Seira, T. 2002. 'Dis-embedding the Sexual/Social Contract: Citizenship and Gender in Nepal'. *Citizenship Studies*, 6(3): 309–324.

Shakya, M. 2018. *Death of an Industry: The Cultural Politics of Garment Manufacturing During the Maoist Revolution in Nepal*. New Delhi: Cambridge University Press.

Shakya, S. 2013. *Unleashing Nepal*. New Delhi: Penguin Books.

Shah, S. 2008. *Civil Society in Uncivil Places: Soft State and Regime Change in Nepal*. Washington DC: East West Center.

Shah, S. 2018. *A Project of Memoreality: Transnational Development and Local Activism*. Kathmandu: Himal Books.

Sharma, J.R. 2008. 'Practices of Male Labor Migration from the Hills of Nepal to India in Development Discourses: Which Pathology?'. *Gender, Technology and Development*, 12(3): 303–323.

Sharma, J.R. 2019. *Crossing the Border to India: Youth, Migration and Masculinities in Nepal*. New Delhi: Bloomsbury.

Sharma, J.R. and A. Donini. 2010. *Towards a "Great Transformation"? The Maoist Insurgency and Local Perceptions of Social Transformation in Nepal*. Tufts University, Medford, MA: Feinstein International Center.

Sharma, J.R. and A. Donini. 2012. *From Subjects to Citizens? Labor, Mobility and Social Transformation in Rural Nepal*. Tufts University, Medford, MA: Feinstein International Center.

Sharma, S. 2019. *Nepal Nexus*. New Delhi: Penguin Books.

Sharrock, J. 2013. 'Stability in Transition: Development Perspectives and Local Politics in Nepal'. *European Bulletin of Himalayan Research*, 42: 9–38.

Shneiderman, S., L. Wagner, J. Rinck, A. Jonson, and A. Lord. 2016. 'Nepal's Ongoing Political Transformation: A Review of Post-2006 Literature on Conflict, the State, Identities, and Environments'. *Modern Asian Studies*, 50(6): 2041–2114.

Simkhada, D. 2017. *Mulukko Muhar, Kathmandu: Social Science Baha.* Kathmandu: Himal Books.

Skerry, C.A., K. Moran, and K.M. Calavan. 1991. *Four Decades of Development: The History of US Assistance to Nepal 1951–1991*. Kathmandu: USAID.

Sob, D. 1997. 'Dalit Women within Oppression'. *Studies in Nepali History and Society*, 2(2): 348–53.

Stewart, F. 2006. 'Do We Need a New "Great Transformation"? Is One Likely?'. *UNU-WIDER Research Paper No. 2006/36*. Helsinki: United Nations University World Institute for Development Economics Research.

Subedi, J. 2016. *British Samrajya ka Nepali Mohara: Gorkha Bhartiko Nalibeli.* Kathmandu: Himal Books.

Sugden, F. 2013. 'Pre-Capitalist Reproduction on the Nepal Tarai: Semifeudal Agriculture in an Era of Globalisation'. *Journal of Contemporary Asia*, 43(3): 519–545.

Sunam, R. 2018. *Sambeshitako Bahas.* Lalitpur: Samata Foundation.

Sunam, R.K. and J.F. McCarthy. 2016. 'Reconsidering the Links between Poverty, International Labour Migration, and Agrarian Change: Critical Insights from Nepal'. *The Journal of Peasant Studies*, 43(1): 39–63.

Thapa, D., ed. 2003. *Understanding the Maoist Movement of Nepal.* Kathmandu: Martin Chautari Centre for Social Research & Development.

Thapa, H.B. 2017. *Rajgaj*. Kathmandu: Fine Print Books.

Thapa, M. 2003. *Rojirotiko Lagi Nepali Shramik Prabasma*. Kathmandu: GEFONT.

The Asia Foundation. 2010. 'Political Economy Analysis of Local Government in Nepal with Special Reference to Education and Health Sectors'. Available at: https://asiafoundation.org/resources/pdfs/analysislocalgovernancenepal.pdf (Accessed on 20 September 2020).

Toffin, G. 2009. 'The Janajati/Adivasi Movement in Nepal: Myths and Realities of Indigeneity'. *Sociological Bulletin*, 58(1): 25–42.

Toffin, G. 2013. *From Monarchy to Republic: Essays in Changing Nepal.* Kathmandu: Vajra Books.

UNESCO. 2019. *UNESCO Institute of Statistics*, UNESCO.

Upadhya, R. 2020. *Cabals and Cartels: An Up-Close Look at Nepal's Turbulent Transition and Disrupted Development.* Kathmandu: Fine Print Books.

Upreti, B.R., S. KC, R. Mallett, and B. Babajanian. 2012. 'Livelihoods, Basic Services and Social Protection in Nepal'. *SLRC Working Paper 7*. London: Secure Livelihoods Research Consortium.

Upretty, P.R. 1992. *Political Awakening in Nepal: The Search for a New Identity*. New Delhi: Commonwealth Publishers.

Vasily, L.A. 2009. 'Struggle against Domination: Forms of Nepali Dalit Activism'. In *Ethnic Activism and Civil Society in South Asia*, edited by D.N. Gellner, 215–238. New Delhi: Sage.

Whelpton, J. 2005. *History of Nepal*. Cambridge: Cambridge University Press.

World Bank. 2018. *Nepal Systematic Country Diagnostic: A New Approach for a Federal Nepal*. World Bank.

Yadav, P. 2016. *Social Transformation in Post-Conflict Nepal: A Gender Perspective*. Oxford and New York: Routledge.

Zharkevich, I. 2019a. *Maoist People's War and the Revolution of Everyday Life in Nepal*. New Delhi: Cambridge University Press.

Zharkevich, I. 2019b. 'Money and Blood: Remittances As a Substance of Relatedness in Transnational Families in Nepal'. *American Anthropologist*, 121(4): 884–896.

People gathered outside a telephone booth to make calls to their family members working away, Doti, 2008.

2

From Subjects to Citizens: Maoist Insurgency and Local Perceptions of Social Change

Previously if they (people of high caste) wanted to talk to us, they would call us and we went to their place. Now they come to where we are. Earlier, they would say—'Oh Rame, come here' and I would simply go (Ye, Rame, yeta aaija ta ani ma khuru khuru janthe). Now, they come to me and say- 'Hello Ram brother or Ramji, I wanted to talk to you about something' (Oho ram bhai or Ram ji, euta sallah garnu parne thiyo). I must say this is a big change, isn't it.

—A Dalit activist in a hill village in western Nepal

They didn't like us wearing good clothes. If they saw you wearing good clothes, they would call you and make you carry dusty bricks. They were very bad. All those days are gone now; the old man is dead.

—A Dalit man in a Terai village in western-central Nepal

Nepal's Maoist insurgency (1996–2005) was built around an agenda for radical change that sought to restructure the very idea of the Nepali state. At its core, the movement attacked the feudal nature of Nepali society and the structural inequalities inherent in it (Hutt 2004). Whether this agenda was instrumental—a tool for capturing power—or represented the aspiration for a profound social revolution remains contentious (Dixit 2009). Nonetheless, the political mobilisation and discourses of the Maoist insurgency did have a notable impact on how people viewed social change around them.

The Maoist agenda, reflected in the 40-point demands charter submitted in 1996 to the then prime minister, Sher Bahadur Deuba, concerned a broad set of questions related to sovereignty, democratic practices and people's livelihoods (Bohara 2002, Rai 2016). In the same year, the Communist Party of Nepal-Maoist (CPN-M) started a rural insurgency in the mid-western hills of Nepal that eventually spread to almost all of the 75 districts (Hutt 2004). The insurgents pursued a classic Maoist strategy of 'encircling the cities', forcing the police and civil servants to retreat to district headquarters (Gersony 2003, Ogura 2008). By mid-2006, over two-thirds of the approximately 4,000 secretaries of Village Development Committees (VDCs)—the lowest tier of government in rural areas—had been relocated to district headquarters or the Nepali Army strongholds (Donini and Sharma 2008). Many VDCs were padlocked, and banks and other state power symbols were blown up or burned, which conferred significant symbolic power on the Maoists. In 2004, when I conducted my doctoral fieldwork in Palpa, the VDC office in the village had been locked by the Maoists for the previous two years. The newly built, whitewashed VDC building was painted by the Maoists with their slogans and demands. A few of the slogans that I read in 2004 were: '*Ne Ka Pa Māobadi Zindābād* (Long live Nepal Communist Party-Maoist) *Asar 28 ko Nepal Band Safal Pārau* (Let's make the Nepal closure of 28 of Asād a success)'; '*Gyane Chor, desh chod* (Gyane—the then King of Nepal—the thief, leave Nepal)'.

The local politicians did not show interest in local-level politics in public and were reluctant to express any political views. The VDC secretary, an official appointed by the government to be stationed in the village, was not in the village, but I met him several times in the district headquarters. The Maoists effectively denied the elected government access and presence throughout rural Nepal. They refused to allow the implementation of hundreds of government-financed roads and water systems, and pressurised the NGOs in their 'base areas' (Shneiderman and Turin 2004). Given that the Nepali state had consolidated its presence and authority through development activities since 1950, as we will discuss in Chapter Five in detail, the expulsion of state-led and state-sanctioned development from the countryside was a key strategy of the Maoists. This demonstrates a contested view the Maoists had on development, that is, while they blocked development activities to challenge the authority of the Nepali state, they were simultaneously promoting alternative development ideas, because power and authority were associated with the idea of development.

Further, the Maoists, in their ideological ambition as well as through patterns of political mobilisation and recruitment, railed against the issues of caste, gender and land-based structural violence inherent in Nepali society. Feudal landlordism and the caste system were challenged through political rhetoric and mobilisations. On questions of land, this manifested in labelling 'landlords' and 'local powerholders' as 'enemies' and targeting them with intimidation and violence. At the local level, the Maoists also introduced, often forcibly, measures aimed at addressing centuries-old deeply rooted forms of discrimination based on caste, ethnicity, gender and class in Nepali rural society. Many class enemies, mainly landlords and, in some cases, teachers and bureaucrats, were forced to leave the rural areas or politically and economically support the insurgency. Parallel 'people's' structures of governance were introduced, and affirmation of caste and ethnic identity was encouraged. Perhaps more profoundly, women's empowerment was promoted through the opposition of social practices, such as relegation during menstruation and childbirth, and the encouragement of women's enrolment in the ranks of the People's Liberation Army and the Maoist governance structures. While the Maoist insurgency brought the questions of exclusion and inequalities into Nepal's public sphere as never before, aspirations and demands for rights and citizenship actually preceded the insurgency. Since the 1950s, different forms of social and political movements, awareness-raising and educational activities have raised questions of inequality and exclusion, and have called for rights and citizenship. Maoist rhetoric and mobilisation must, therefore, be placed in this historical context of calls for change.

Based on local perceptions of social transformation during the decade of Maoist insurgency and the political transition following it, this chapter focuses on Nepal's transformation from a deeply feudal and hierarchical society to one where ideas of rights and citizenship are pervasive. Perceptions, of course, do not always match 'reality'. What this chapter explores is more about judgments about the transformation and how ordinary people have related to, engaged with and been impacted by these changes, and what local people considered meaningful to themselves. It outlines the major shifts underway in Nepali society in terms of ideas of rights and citizenship, which broadly correspond to the Nepali state's political transformation from absolute monarchy to constitutional monarchy and then to a republican state. The chapter makes the argument that the combination of social and political mobilisations under the guises of Maoist insurgency, ethnic and regional social movements, in parallel with significant legal, constitutional and institutional changes, the development of formal and non-formal education and the opening up of the market and the public sphere(s), has resulted in a historical transformation of consciousness. Awareness of rights and ideas of equality has increased massively; the collective agency of women and oppressed and marginalised groups has escalated and has resulted in notable changes in how individuals, groups and institutions interrelate.

Following this introduction, the next section gives a brief background of Nepal's political history. The following section, then, describes the local perceptions of the nature and drivers of social change, drawing on the interviews and discussions with local people. After presenting what was meaningful to people, this chapter concludes with a brief analysis of what these perceptions of social change tell us about the nature of social transformation more broadly.

A Brief History of Nepal's Compressed Political Transition

By any standard, Nepal's political transformation is dramatic. Notably, between 2006 and 2015, through the peace process, Nepal transitioned from a Hindu to a secular state, from monarchy to republicanism and from a highly centralised to a federal state (Jha 2014, Sharma 2019). More fundamentally, the new constitutional order has enabled it to shift from an exclusive state, controlled by a dominant minority, to a state that has sought to be inclusive by adapting to its diversity, as well as by embedding a framework of human rights, equality and citizenship.

Multi-layered exclusion based on caste, ethnicity, gender and class has been central to the history of nation-state formation in Nepal (Gellner et al. 1997, Lawoti 2005). Ruled by Hindu Kings and Ranas for over 200 years, the Nepali state has been dominated by what some social scientists have called 'Parbatiyas', that is, members of the Nepali-speaking high caste groups, from the hills (Gellner et al. 1997, Lawoti 2005). Historically, this dominance was enabled by King Prithvi Narayan Shah's nation-building process, which started from the mid-hills. Before 1769, Nepal was divided into many autonomous petty states. King Prithvi Narayan Shah and his successors started integrating Nepal into a single nation with the ambition of establishing *asal Hindustan* or true Hindu land (Whelpton 2005). The Parbatiyas were closely aligned with the ruling Shah elites and benefitted from access to power. In turn, the Shah rulers tried to maintain a puritanical Hindu character, one distinct from India, then ruled by the Muslim Moghuls. This institutional legacy has been divisive. Although the dominant Nepali nationalists continue to feel proud of the moves of Prithvi Narayan Shah, who is known as the founder of the Nepali nation, and his successors towards creating a greater Nepal and strategically resisting the external threat, his critics see his aim to create *asal Hindustan* as a way of marginalising the non-Hindu ethnic groups (Gurung 1997, Whelpton 2005).

In 1846, while the Shah kings were still the rulers, de facto control came under the Ranas, who ruled for 104 years as hereditary prime ministers (1846–1950). Given the persistent external threat from an expanding British Empire, the Rana rulers allowed Nepal to be a semi-colony of the British Empire and got exposed to the intricacies of the British rule (Blaikie et al. 1980). One of the key developments during the Rana regime was the Muluki Ain (National Code), enforced in 1854, which legitimised the caste system, gender hierarchy and superiority of the Hindu religion (Whelpton 2005, Aahuti 2010). The Muluki Ain institutionalised a caste-based social order, where diverse castes and ethnic categories were incorporated into a single national caste hierarchy that privileged high-caste Hindus and marginalised people of lower castes, or those outside the caste hierarchies, such as Dalits and non-Hindu Janajati groups (Pfaff-Czarnecka, 1997). Although the concept of the code is said to be inspired by western ideas, following the visit of the Rana prime minister, Jung Bahadur, to Europe, the content reflected the interests of dominant elites. Overall, the pre-1951 rulers put Nepal under a Hindu ritual framework. For the rulers, the plurality of Nepali society was conceived of within-the-uniform socio-political framework. Rather than seeking to establish national unity through a vision of a culturally homogeneous population, the rulers sought to define a national identity, which allowed for cultural variation, but had Hinduism as its major pillar (Pfaff-Czarnecka 1997, 425–426).

The year 1950, when the 104-year-old hereditary Rana rule came to an end, marked a significant political change in Nepal's history. It was replaced by a short-lived experiment with multiparty democracy with constitutional monarchy from 1951 to 1960, and then by three decades of a party-less panchayat system led by King Mahendra, and then by his brother, King Birendra. When India became independent from British rule in 1947, and the Rana regime subsequently ended, there was a massive aspiration for democracy, development and progress. The aspiration for development was supported heavily by foreign aid, and it closely resonated with the aspiration of newly independent countries elsewhere. Development, supported by foreign aid from different countries, became a major modernising force during the Panchayat era. Unlike the Rana era, as summarised above by Pfaff-Czarnecka, the Shah rulers attempted to promote the notion of one nation sharing a common culture in the post-1951 era. Their major strategies were: equality of citizens under the law (although, as we discuss below, the caste system was not explicitly abolished), a modern administrative system, conduct of elections, welcoming of foreign aid and a project of modern development aimed at turning former subjects into citizens or *nagarik*.

The end of the Rana regime did result in significant legal and institutional changes. For the first time in Nepal's history, the Interim Government of Nepal Act (1951) and Nepal's Constitution of 1959 explicitly prohibited the government from discriminating against any citizen in the application of law or appointment to government service on the grounds of religion, ethnicity, caste, gender and place of birth (Pradhan 2005). The new modern vision of the Nepali state did not discriminate against its citizens in the application of law or employment in the state sector. Despite this, the Muluki Ain continued to support the caste-based Hindu hierarchical system (Whelpton 2005). After short-lived experimentation with multiparty democracy, in 1961, King Mahendra overthrew the elected government, instituted the panchayat political system and established himself as an absolute monarch. The new Constitution of 1962 and the new Muluki Ain of 1963 regarded all Nepalis as citizens and not as individuals belonging to a particular caste or ethnicity (Pfaff-Czarnecka 1997).

During the three decades of the Panchayat period, the ruling elite, which consisted mainly of high caste *Parbatiyas*, attempted to implement the ideals of a homogeneous nation-state identity based on a shared culture (Parbatiya), religion (Hindu) and language (Nepali) (Pfaff-Czarnecka 1997). Euphemised by slogans like 'one nation, one language and one people', the government attempted to promote the Nepali language as the lingua franca and the only medium of instruction in schools (Pfaff-Czarnecka 1997). Similarly, the census was designed to show the numerical dominance of Hindus in Nepal by classifying even some non-Hindu ethnic groups as Hindus (Pradhan 2005). Further, Nepali nationalism sought to exaggerate the differences with India. This nationalism, which rested on anti-Indianness, particularly disadvantaged Madhesis living in the southern plains in the Nepal–India borderland, who share cultural, linguistic kinship and economic ties across the border and whose loyalty to the Nepali nation has always been doubted by the Nepali nationalists (ICG 2007). Such virulent nationalism also exhibited itself in the legal regime on citizenship. The Nepal Citizenship Act was promulgated in 1964 and institutionalised single citizenship for the entire population beyond their caste or ethnic identity (ICG 2007). It had both residency-related criteria and that of proficiency in oral and written skills in the Nepali language. This provision directly disadvantaged and excluded many Madhesis, who spoke non-Nepali languages, and were likely to fail on strict residency grounds (ICG 2007).

The 'developmental' aspiration of the Panchayat period also led to substantial social engineering in Nepal's Terai, which directly impacted the indigenous Tharus. As we will discuss in Chapter Five, a massive malaria-control programme, supported by USAID, was implemented in the Terai, leading to the clearance of dense forest and encouragement of hill migrants to settle in different parts of the Terai (Gunaratne 1998, Robertson 2018). It would appear that King Mahendra manipulated the threat of the malaria epidemic, Malthusian fear of population, environmental degradation and food insecurity in his favour by encouraging the settlement of the people of hill origin in the Terai as a way to counter what he saw as a threat to Nepali nationalism from Indian immigrants in Terai.

Beyond the politics of language, culture and religion, the idea of the Nepali nation and Nepali citizens was intensely promoted primarily through development policies and activities. In its efforts to promote nationalism based on cultural unity, the government mobilised the concept of *bikas*, the provision of physical infrastructure such as roads and air transport, radio and educational and administrative systems privileging the Nepali language over others (Gyawali 2018). Such nationalist politics resonated with the aspirations of newly independent countries to modernise their economy, politics and society. Yet, continuing from the Rana era, a culture of nepotism (*aafno manche*[1]) and subservience (*chakari*[2]) was common in the bureaucracy (Bista 1991). Literacy and educational programmes were a key part of the development strategy. The objective of education, both schooling and literacy programmes, was about getting rid of cultural obstacles that hindered 'progress'. Government-supported literacy programmes aimed at imparting basic literacy skills and raising awareness through Freirean pedagogy. Many NGOs used literacy programmes as a way to access local communities and begin their community organisation work.

As a way to shield the political system from the dissent that was silently brewing, the Panchayat period had instituted severe restrictions on freedom and human rights (Baral 1977). The state did not allow human rights organisations to operate and prohibited political activities. Law and order were maintained through a strict administrative system under Chief District Officers and Zonal Administrators, who reported directly to the palace secretariat. Control of access to information, along with state propaganda, was maintained

1 A form of sycophancy common in the Nepali bureaucracy for job security, transfer and promotion (See, Justice 1986, Bista 1991).

2 Literally translates to one's own people, inner circle or nepotism (*See*, Subedi 2014, Bista, 1991).

through Radio Nepal and state-run newspapers. Any limited dissent from human rights and political activists only existed underground.

The restoration of multiparty democracy in 1990 successfully ended the 30 years of Panchayat rule and enabled the transition to a Constitutional monarchy under a multiparty system. A new era of democratisation, multiculturalism, egalitarianism and expansion of the public sphere now existed in Nepal like never before. The year 1990 marked yet another critical juncture for change. Article 11 of the Constitution of 1991 granted equal rights to all citizens before the law and prohibited any form of discrimination based on religion, race (*barna*), caste (*jat*) or ethnicity (*jati*). Unlike the Panchayat system, the new constitution declared Nepal a multi-ethnic, multilingual, constitutional monarchical kingdom.

The fundamental rights guaranteed by the new constitution enabled significant growth and proliferation of different media, civil society, ethnic, professional and non-governmental organisations (NGOs), which have transformed the character of Nepal's public sphere (Onta 2002). Whereas the government during the Panchayat era monopolised Radio Nepal, there was a media boom in the years after 1990, as newspapers, FM stations and TV channels multiplied, offering different perspectives from across the political spectrum (Onta 2002).

Opening up of the public sphere allowed the surfacing of long-standing grievances on cultural, linguistic and ethnic grounds. Many caste-based and ethnic organisations were established to preserve and seek recognition of their culture and heritage, and to demand representation and a share of economic and political benefits. By using the term *Janajati* explicitly in Article 26(10), the new Constitution acknowledged their presence and relative deprivation in social and economic terms (Onta 2006). Although the Janajati movement had a long history (Fisher 1993), in the post-1990 era, the movement was institutionalised and consolidated under the Nepal Janajati Mahasangh or the Nepal Federation of Ethnic Nationalities (NEFEN). It was later renamed as the Nepal Federation of Indigenous Nationalities (NEFIN) to align their struggle with the international language on indigeneity and cultural rights. The movement aims to challenge the exclusionary and extractive nature of the Nepali state, dominated by Nepali-speaking high-caste Hindus, and create a vision of an inclusive Nepal as a multi-ethnic, multilinguistic and multireligious state in which 'discrimination against ethnic groups does not exist' (Onta 2006, Hagen 2010).

Since the issues raised by the movement reflected global ideas of equality, rights, justice, democracy, participation and development (*bikas*), the movement was able to draw wider attention and strengthen mobilisation through financial, technical and political support from international donors (Sharma 2012). As the demands of the Janajatis gained strength during the 1990s and early 2000s, the Nepali government responded with various initiatives to address those demands by creating state institutions to look into the Janajatis' issues.

While the Adivasi Janajati assertion has received significant scholarly attention, social and political movements in this period were not limited to ethnic movements, but included other groups, such as professional associations, NGOs, CBOs and local user groups. Both formally and informally, grassroots mobilisations began through these organisations and opened up space for deliberative and organic democracy. There were several social movements and NGOs campaigning for freedom for bonded labourers such as Kamaiyas and Haliyas, as well as other movements for the rights of Dalits, children, women and third gender, among others. For example, a notable NGO working in women's rights and anti-trafficking, Maiti Nepal, was established in 1993, and the Backward Society Education (BASE), fighting against bonded labour, was established in 1990. Child Workers in Nepal Concerned Centre (CWIN), a major child welfare and rights NGO formed in 1985 by a group of left-leaning human rights activists, initially provided a day care centre for street children, but then graduated to be a leading NGO championing child rights and raising questions on child labour and children's and women's rights.

The complexities and dynamics of gender, caste, ethnicity and class in Nepali society have been well documented (Gellner 2007). As indicated above, in the post-1990 era, the public sphere in Nepal witnessed the emergence and rapid growth of various forms of social movements claiming recognition and activities of NGOs working on a range of social development issues. However, compared to wider South Asia, social movements calling for distributions of resources and goods have been non-existent; they have been less debated academically and have been marginal in the policy community. In the absence of questions of distribution of resources and goods, it is alleged that social scientists working in the region failed to see the possibility of a Maoist insurgency in Nepal. Only two scholars, Andrew Nickson (1992) and Stephan L. Mikesell (1993), wrote about the potential for a Peruvian Shining Path-style Maoist uprising in Nepal (Gellner 2007). Therefore, the Maoist insurgency and movement of former bounded labourers brought redistribution issues to the fore. Although the Maoist insurgency began as a movement mobilising peasants in rural Nepal, over the years the Maoists have tacitly attracted support from other identity-based movements including those mobilising Adivasi Janajati, and other minority groups and, thus, relegating issues of redistribution to the backburner.

While the Maoist movement brought about sea-changes in Nepali polity and society and mainstreamed inclusion and state-restructuring agendas, it was Nepal's historic and protracted peace process that consolidated these agendas, giving it a constitutional mandate. Against the authoritarianism unleashed by King Gyanendra, between 2001 and 2005, there was an alliance between different democratic political parties, grouped as the Seven Party Alliance (SPA), who were agitating against the King and the Maoists in a bid to restore democracy. Facilitated by India, the alliance and the bargains between the SPA and the Maoists took the shape of a 12-point agreement. At the heart of the agreement was the SPA's acceptance of the Maoist demands to elect a Constituent Assembly. This Assembly would write a new constitution to form a basis for 'restructuring of the state', based on federalism and republicanism while the Maoists would renounce violence and accept multiparty democracy (Martin 2012). With the peace process, the Maoists had transitioned from a small political movement with limited support in the western hills (Gersony 2003), to one of the major players in Nepali politics (Hachethu 2009). A joint movement of the Maoists and the SPA, the people's movement, which garnered popular support, and international legitimacy, also brought down the 240-year-old monarchy. Building on the 12-point agreement, a Comprehensive Peace Accord (CPA) was signed between the parties, paving the way for an institutionalised peace process. The CPA committed to carrying out 'an inclusive, democratic and progressive restructuring of the state by ending the current centralised and unitary form of the state in order to address the problems related to women, Dalits, indigenous people, Janajati, Madhesi, oppressed, neglected and minority communities and backward regions by ending discrimination based on class, caste, language, gender, culture, religion and region' (Government of Nepal and Community Party of Nepal, Maoists 2006). The CPA paved the way for an Interim Constitution and an Interim Government with the Maoists participating in it in April 2007. In line with the CPA, as per the request of the government and Maoists, the Security Council also mandated the establishment of the UN mission in Nepal (UNMIN) in early 2007 (Dixit 2009, Martin 2012).

While the Maoist conflict was being settled, new identity-based mobilisations were erupting. The promulgation of the Interim Constitution of 2007 promoted major civil unrest in the Terai led by Madhesi activists. Originating on the pretext that the Constitution had failed to make any specific mention of federalism, the movement has been central in making federalism a cardinal issue in Nepali politics (Gautam 2008). While federalism has been a key demand of the Madhesi and Janajati activists and the Maoists (who had tactically supported it), post-2007, the articulation of this demand became fiercer, as Madhesis and Janajati activists took to the streets. The movement spurred an amendment to Nepal's Interim Constitution of 2007. Federalism accompanied other wide-ranging policies for inclusion in the Constitution, including access for excluded groups to state organs based on proportional inclusion. More importantly, the Madhesi protests of 2007 led to the emergence of regional political parties in Nepal. As various identity groups put forward their demands, often contradictory to each other, the state continued to sign agreements with agitating groups as a way to prevent violent conflict, regardless of its genuine commitment or capacity to address them.

Following the spirit of the CPA, the Government of Nepal amended Civil Service Act (2049) and adopted the policy of reservations. According to this amendment, 45 per cent of the seats in Nepal's civil service has been reserved for different marginalised groups, that is, 33 per cent for women, 27 per cent for Adivasi Janajatis, 22 per cent for Madhesis, 9 per cent for Dalits, 5 per cent for disabled and 4 per cent for those from backward regions. Likewise, in response to the CPA, an election for the Constituent Assembly was held in 2008. The elections saw the Maoist emerge as the biggest party, along with different Madhesi-based parties, which fared reasonably well. The inclusion-related provisions in the Interim Constitution, and more specifically, a mixed electoral system, with around 60 per cent allocated to a proportional representation system, elected the most diverse and inclusive parliament in Nepal's history. The challenge posed by the Maoists and Madhesi parties to the old political order dominated by traditional parties like the Nepali Congress as well as the Unified Marxist–Leninist (UML) party, along with the movement for inclusion, upsetting the composition of state structures, fomented slow-burn reprisals against the inclusion agenda. The Constitution writing that began in 2008, with repeated extensions of the Constitution Assembly, was mired in disagreements between the parties on modalities and the scope of federalism. Moreover, the provision for the management of arms and armaments, which sought to verify former Maoist combatants, disarm them and either integrate them within the Nepal Army or rehabilitate them back into society was also a point of great contention (Dixit 2009, Jha 2014, Sharma 2019). While provisions on the management of arms and armament were worked out in 2012, with the integration of 1460 Maoist fighters into the Nepali Army and different rehabilitation-related schemes offered to the rest, agreement on modalities of federalism continued to be a sticking point. Unable to agree on these and given the stark differences between those supporting the ethnicity-based federalism demanded by Janajati members and Maoists, and other parties who wanted federalism to be largely an exercise of administrative devolution, the tenure of the CA expired and was dissolved in 2012. This event was followed by a new round of elections in 2013. In contrast to the electoral balance sheet of 2007, in 2013, the NC and UML emerged as the largest and the second-largest political forces, while the Maoists and Madhesis, who championed the revolutionary vision of Nepali state structure, had a reduced electoral mandate. Despite changes in the CA and its composition, the disagreement on federalism persisted.

This constitutional turbulence was only to be settled against the backdrop of the Nepal earthquake of April 2015, which had a major impact on the need for consensus for constitution writing. In a bid to cater to the exigencies of the rebuilding process, a 16-point agreement between four major political parties (NC, UML, Maoist and Madhesi Janadhikar Forum-Loktantrik) resolved the contentious issue of federalism. The agreement decided on pertinent issues, including the number of provinces, naming of provinces and the process of federal demarcation. This agreement between political parties, however, reduced the space for deliberations at the CA. Further, this fast-tracking of the Constitution writing process, based on an agreement outside the CA, meant little public debate on the issue. The new Constitution, with its provincial boundaries, faced significant protests and resistance from the Madhesis who had long campaigned for one Madhesi province across the southern plains of Nepal. The Constitution regressed on multiple commitments enshrined in the 2007 Constitution. For example, it subverted citizenship rights for women from the 2006 Citizenship Act, and the rights women had gained concerning passing on citizenship to their children. The turn to secularism was diluted, with secularism redefined to include the practice of Hinduism, and the status of the cow as the national animal was maintained. Further, the provisions for affirmative action, which had an immediate bearing on the increased participation of marginalised groups in state institutions, were weakened. Due to protests from the dominant group, Khas Arya was included among the groups eligible for affirmative action, defeating the very purpose of affirmative action. The ratio between the two electoral systems First-Past-The-Post (FTTP) and Proportional Representation (PR) was changed from 44:56 to 60:40. Overall, the new constitution limited the number of progressive gains made in the initial years of the peace process. Despite these limitations, the political changes have opened new institutional avenues, including reservations for excluded groups in all state institutions and the civil service, as well as organisational levels in the major political parties (Rai 2020). In the first decade since the amendment of the Civil Service Act (2049 BS) in 2007, a total of 14,814 applicants benefitted from reservations policy (Sunam 2018). An analysis shows that a third of all women (5,217 out of 16,385), and a fourth of all Madhesis (3,226 out of 13,172 Madhesis), Adivasi Janajati (4,004 out of 16,638) and a significant proportion of Dalits (1,347 out of 1,733) in Nepal's civil service benefitted from the reservations policy (Sunam 2018). Quotas have also been instituted in elections to all three tiers of government—federal, provincial and municipal—to generate gender and caste equality (Thapa 2019). At the local government level, one of the party candidates for the top two posts has to be a woman and, at the lowest tier of the government, at the ward level, of the four members, at least two must be women, one of whom has to be a Dalit (Thapa 2019).

By any standard, this compressed political transformation has been radical. How are these macro-political transformations and their agendas of change reflected in local people's perceptions? Beyond the popular debate on state restructuring at the national level, how do ordinary people view radical social change agendas? The next section reflects on local perceptions of the discourses of social change.

Local Perceptions of the Dynamics of Social Change

The following section describes the people's perceptions and views on the nature and drivers of change, drawing on interviews and discussions with local people. As described below, local people's perceptions of social change themes reflect the major patterns of inequalities and structural violence in Nepal (Blaikie et al. 1980; DFID/World Bank 2006).

Caste and Untouchability

During my fieldwork, participants interchangeably used the term *tallo jaat* or Dalit. The former means lower caste. The word 'Dalit' means oppressed and is adopted from the Dalit movement in India. It is used as a collective identity of all the 'untouchable' caste groups into one, so that they can collectively reject the hierarchically organised ritual pollution and injustice embedded in the caste system. There was a high level of consciousness among the Dalits of their social position. A new sense of Dalit identity was visible in rural areas. People frequently identified themselves as Dalits, and not necessarily their occupational names, like Damai, Kami, Sarki and Gaine. In the group discussions and meetings, both men and women introduced themselves with their full names and added 'Dalit bata' (meaning from the oppressed-caste group). The growth of public meetings in the villages often organised by NGOs or CBOs meant that the formal practice of introducing participants had expanded in collective gatherings, and such meetings provided a space to assert Dalit identity.

Caste-based discrimination had become a significant and sensitive public issue in the communities. It was obvious that people had become more political, and it had become easier for Dalits to confront non-Dalits when they felt discriminated against. Referring to the historical upper-caste dominance in his village, a young man in a hill village in western Nepal said, 'The situation is not like before, now we don't keep quiet'. Dalits felt that the Maoists' political mobilisations during and after the insurgency years had provided them with a space to enjoy their rights. 'Whatever we may say about the Maoists, they did raise our issue', said a Dalit woman in a hill village in western Nepal. She put it, 'The Maoists say we are all equal; there are only two castes: man and woman.' Dalits felt that the changing political context and the popularity of the Maoists had provided them with a space to assert their rights. Young Dalit men and women had a higher level of self-esteem and the confidence to complain against injustice. They had begun to speak for themselves and build social and political networks. Dalit mobilisation, with the support of NGOs, had reached village households in all the areas.

In a Terai village in the western central region, men from a lower-caste background often greeted outside visitors with 'lal salam' (red salute) and said that Maoists had done a great job by providing them with a 'citizenship card' denied to them previously by the state, which claimed they were recent migrants from India. A Dalit middle-aged man in a Terai village shared that he had been denied a citizenship card until very recently. He felt he had been denied his right to citizenship because of his background (that is, a *harijan* from the Terai). He felt that the Maoists had provided people like him with citizenship (*nagarikta*) and justice (*nyaya*).

Perhaps what this middle-aged Dalit woman said best reflects the nature of the transformation in caste relations in contemporary rural Nepal: 'Earlier, people used to call us "Damai" (tailor caste) and looked down at us and spoke to us in an authoritative voice; these days, they call us Dalit. It is different. Their language has become softer, at least in public.' Such perceptions of dignity and respect indicate a shift in inter-caste relations.

There have been visible and significant changes in the caste domain, including increased agency of Dalits and proliferation of Dalit identity movements at the local level, social mobility among Dalits and a notable change in aspects of caste-based discrimination. Indicating a difficult battle, a Dalit activist who managed a local NGO in western Nepal opined that it was difficult to change people's attitudes, especially older Dalits and non-Dalits. He said, 'It is easy to educate people who are ignorant about something, but it is very difficult to work with people who already know.' There is direct and indirect resistance from the upper caste. An upper-caste teacher in the Terai commented, 'Dalits can now go to the temple ... but they don't know how to pray.' Despite the impressive assertion of rights, such a demeaning attitude towards Dalits continues.

Dalit men and women proudly said that they were addressed by their name with respect, and there was no use of abusive or discriminatory language. A Dalit woman from a hill village commented, 'They call us by name and treat us with respect in front; I don't know what they do behind our back.' Upper-caste men and women said that they used respectful language while speaking to Dalits. An upper-caste man said, 'These days, if we show a little bit of carelessness, they will create fire. We have to be extremely careful. Maybe our fathers and grandfathers treated them with less respect; I don't think we do that.' He felt that now people had become 'aware' that all are equal and attributed this change to education. Referring to the 'new political climate' favouring the 'lower-caste population', Dalit men opined that it was almost impossible for people from high castes to treat them with disrespect.

Generally speaking, there was a significant difference between the perceptions of high-caste people, many of whom denied there was any significant discrimination against Dalits remaining in their communities, and Dalits, who felt that despite some major changes, various forms of discrimination against lower-caste communities continued. Dalits throughout the fieldwork areas had become 'aware' that they had been historically discriminated against and maintained the belief that the upper caste had exploited them. Indeed, there was a strong sense of resentment against the upper caste. There was a common perception among the upper caste and Dalits that caste-based discrimination had decreased significantly in the last couple of decades. The practice of untouchability had decreased in public places (*sarbajanik thau*). However, there were hardly any changes in the private sphere (*ghar bhitra*), that is, eating together or being invited inside each other's houses or inter-caste marriages.

Observation showed that both Dalits and non-Dalits participated in public meetings or met for discussions in local tea shops. However, it was possible to identify Dalits and non-Dalits as they often sat in separate groups. As a young Dalit man in a Terai village in western Nepal put it, 'We had some money from VDC to do something. So, last week we had a Dalit awareness programme in the village. People from high caste came and gave wonderful speeches. They said this *thulo jati* (upper caste) and *sano jati* (lower caste) are all "purano soch" (old thinking), we are in new Nepal, etc. But, when the programme was over, they sat together and had samosas, they didn't eat with us.' He added, 'That is exactly what I call *bahunbad* (Brahmanism). The situation was different when they travelled outside their villages, often to take part in activities sponsored by NGOs or political parties, where both Dalits and non-Dalits were seen sitting and eating together.

Dalit men and women could drink tea or eat in restaurants/shops owned by higher castes. Similarly, men from higher castes often ate in shops owned by Dalits. Unlike previously, Dalit men did not have to wash their dishes after use in restaurants and tea shops. In a far western hill village, Dalits had begun to keep buffalos and sell milk, which was prohibited in the past. In former times, the practice was forbidden as high-caste people would not buy their milk. In several towns, Dalits could enter the temple, which had been proscribed. Although this practice was resisted by the high caste and a strong sense of resentment was present among the high caste in the towns, consistent local Dalit activism supported by NGOs and political networks had sustained the change.

Dalits had begun to abandon many practices associated with patronage based on the caste system. A few upper-caste men and women said that they did not discriminate against Dalits because of their caste, but commented that they lacked cleanliness and culture. Many upper-caste men and women often demeaned Sarkis (leather workers) for eating *sino* (meat of dead animals). As a response to such comments and allegations, Sarkis had abandoned the practice of eating *sino*.

In the hills of western Nepal, Dalits have stopped respecting the *bali ghare* system, a system of attached labour based on the caste system. *Bali ghare* required Sarkis (leather workers), Damais (tailors), Kamis (ironworkers) and Gaines (singers) to provide annual services for upper-caste people in their villages and, in return, they received grains and gifts on an annual basis. *Bali ghare* was not paid based on the daily or hourly service. In many ways, feudal attitudes and practices have been challenged. However, such change is not uniform. Mushaharis (Terai Dalits) and some Tharus in the Terai continued to work under feudal conditions for their 'owners', that is, the upper-caste landlords.

There was a widespread perception among the upper caste in the village that things were changing and they were losing control and power over Dalits. As a response, a few high-caste men and women made sarcastic remarks about lower-caste people for their active agency in challenging upper-caste dominance in the last 8–10 years. 'These days, we have to be extremely conscious of what we say; people are looking for opportunities. They are very reactive,' commented a Chettri man in a far-western hill village.

Very few Dalits practised caste-based occupations. Except for a few individuals, Damais (tailoring caste) were not working as tailors, Kamis (iron smiths) were not seen making agricultural and household tools and Sarkis (leather workers) were not producing shoes and other leather products. There was a widespread perception that it was cheaper and easier (and more fashionable) to buy ready-made Chinese clothes. Markets were full of cheap plastic and aluminium utensils. Shoes and bags of different designs and colours were available in the market. Similarly, with the popularity and spread of Dalit movements, there was a general push to abandon traditional occupations based on the caste-system. Likewise, very few upper-caste Bahuns were seen working as priests; the young Bahuns did not want to work as priests, as the profession had been challenged by Dalits and ethnic activists and ridiculed in the recent years.

One of the most significant changes has been the growth in schooling among Dalits. Citing the examples of successful Dalits who completed their schooling and found salaried employment, several Dalits emphasised that it was the lack of education that had put them at a disadvantage. In recent years, we were told, more Dalit men and women had completed their studies and had been recruited by NGOs, the civil service and the private sector in the cities. In many villages, we saw Dalit families who valued education and felt empowered by it. Often these families seemed to be more self-assured and upwardly mobile than impoverished upper-caste families.

Generally speaking, people (both Dalit and non-Dalit women and men) agreed that both formal and informal education had played an essential role in bringing about this change. The growth in schooling and participation in various forms of non-formal education classes, run by the state or NGOs, had made people 'aware' and were considered a crucial vector of transformation. The NGOs that worked on social justice were given credit for mobilising communities on the matter of caste discrimination, which had played a central role in raising Dalit consciousness. Maoists were often given credit for providing justice to Dalits when there had been instances of caste-based discrimination in local communities. Upper-caste people who did not support the Maoists felt that the Dalits had become very powerful in the villages with Maoist support.

In a departure from the past, Dalits came out openly to participate in different community activities. There was a higher level of participation of Dalits in local committees and local political issues. In all community affairs, there was a Dalit quota, and educated Dalit men and women made efforts to ensure that it was maintained, although it did not necessarily mean that Dalits could alter the decision making. In all the local institutions, including schools and health posts, there was Dalit representation, and NGO support was often instrumental here.

Dalits felt that, despite new provisions on quota systems in electoral and administrative structures, they did not have the networks or economic or political power to turn major decisions in their favour. Overall, ritualistic aspects of caste-discrimination in terms of purity and pollution had been challenged, at least in the public sphere, although upper castes still held significant economic and political power.

Gender Discrimination and Women's Position

Women across different caste, ethnic and class groups had become increasingly 'aware' of gender-based discrimination and spoke about 'women's rights'. Men opined that discrimination against women was still a problem in their communities, but felt that things had changed considerably in the last 15–20 years. Women who had access to schooling and those who took part in various social and political activities in the communities in the form of public meetings organised by NGOs, and government and political parties were more vocal about gender-based discrimination against women. In rural Nepal, there has been the emergence of a new cadre of women who work as volunteers (*swayam sewika*), facilitators (*sahajkarta*) or community mobilisers (*samudaik parichalak*) for NGOs or development programmes. However, most women had limited opportunities to participate in these various sociopolitical activities and had low levels of awareness of their rights. When we asked a Chettri woman, aged 45, in a hill village in western Nepal, if she knew about women's rights, she told us that she was not educated and asked us to approach other women in her village. She said, 'People like me do not understand these things (*ma yesto kura bujhdina*), you should ask other women who understand these things (*kura bujhne mahila*).' Another woman continued, 'They go to meetings, they go to cities, they do a lot of different things, they say women's rights ... I never went to school ... my fate is to carry fodder and firewood.' In her view, there were two types of women in her village, that is, those who understand (*kura bujhne*) and those who do not understand (*kura naujhne*).

One of the most visible changes in the last two decades was that an increasing number of girl children went to school in the villages. Both women and men felt that this was a significant change in their communities in the last two to three decades. As a result, some girls had begun to study in a nearby town or a city and take up salaried employment within the village or in nearby towns.

Women spoke about the discrimination faced by women in Nepal and articulated their right to be treated equally. A young Dalit girl in the Terai, aged 20, who worked as a clerk in a government office, said, 'Women have long been discriminated against, and we are still treated as second-class citizens (*doshro darja ko nagarik*) ... but the situation is changing; women are getting educated.' Despite a heightened sense of discrimination, women on their own did not always feel comfortable talking about the problems they faced. However, in public meetings and group discussions, they did speak openly and often with a radical tone, about their discrimination by the state, society and their households. Space for collective meetings created by NGOs and CBOs provided women with a sense of agency. For instance, a Tharu woman from a Terai village found it extremely difficult to talk about the situation of women in her village when a local field assistant (female) attempted to interview her. However, she spoke openly in the discussions when she was a part of the group. Similarly, women felt that schooling practices among younger women and various literacy and non-formal education classes had impacted women's confidence and self-esteem considerably.

Increased confidence and self-esteem among women had resulted in women participating in various campaigns to address problems in their communities. The cases of domestic violence and neglect of women within the households had become public issues. Women collectively dealt with domestic violence incidents and intervened on behalf of abused women or reported the problem to police with the support of NGOs. Women and men said that Maoists would punish men in public who beat their wives, although this did not always happen.

In several areas, local women's groups played a significant role in the banning of uncontrolled sale and public abuse of alcohol. We were told that women often spilt the liquor and put restrictions on alcohol production. Such incidents were often reported on FM radios or in newspapers, and the news circulated rapidly. Women involved in these protests claimed that domestic violence had decreased considerably, and there was strong support from the Maoists for their activities.

Another related activity was women taking a collective role in stopping gambling (playing cards) among men. Typically, a group of 15–20 women would enter the gambling venue, burn the cards and give a warning to the men. Alongside the women, the Maoists were active in stopping gambling. In many instances, the Maoists' tactics to stop gambling included forcing the players to eat their cards, which was humiliating, and declaring non-gambling zones.

In western Nepal, traditional practices, like the Chaupadi system, were challenged, if not completely forbidden. In the Chaupadi system, women were considered polluted and were required to sleep in the cowshed (or a similar hut known as *chaupadi*) during menstruation and during childbirth. Increased understanding of the dangers of this practice has been largely attributed to the awareness-raising work of NGOs and CBOs.

The concept of pollution has been challenged. Women are allowed to give birth within the house and not in the cowshed as had been practised earlier in some areas. Although most participants acknowledged that some form of pollution was still observed, that is, during menstruation, women have to stay in a separate room and observe pollution practices while eating. Education and massive public health programmes were cited as the most important drivers of change. However, education could not result in complete abandonment of age-old practices relating to the observation of pollution in women.

There was a general agreement that both formal and informal education played an important role in increasing 'awareness' on the issue of poor representation and participation of women in society. Rama, a middle-aged Bahun woman who often took part in NGO activities in a hill village in western Nepal, said, 'Women are now educated, (their) level of awareness in society has increased significantly ... it is because of education (*sikcha*) ... the situation has changed a lot. These days women are not passive; they come out to take part in meetings and groups.' When we asked her how the situation had changed, she replied, 'It is education (*sikcha*); the radio keeps telling not to discriminate against girl children ... in our village, you won't find a single girl child who does not go to school ... we organised various meetings, went door to door ... people from outside came (NGO workers) and gave us training (*talim haru*) to send girls to school.'

The activities of NGOs and CBOs, including meetings and training, played an essential role in creating public awareness and pushing the issue of gender balance and representation at the community level. 'NGOs bring various programmes to empower women; some bring programmes on saving groups (*bachat samuha*); others bring programmes on mothers' groups (*ama samuha*) and forest groups (*ban samuha*) ... they give education and teach us,' said a Dalit woman in a Terai village in western Nepal.

There has been a significant change in women's participation in various social and political activities in the last decade. It is now possible to observe meetings of mothers' groups and saving groups. In a village in eastern Terai, 30 women had gathered at 9 AM for their monthly saving meeting. All the women (married and mostly between the ages of 20 and 40) were able to take time out from their household chores to participate in this activity for not less than two hours. All the women members came together to make savings, and selected women took credit for various income-generating activities. We could see women participants holding money (up to रु500) in the meeting. The meeting involved calculating the group's savings and working collectively to ensure repayment of the loan. Towards the end of the meeting, women collectively read the 'prayer' (*prarthana*) written on the back of their savings booklet, which stated their commitment to work collectively for saving and social development. Though these women were able to come for these meetings, their responsibilities at home had not changed. They returned to their homes after the meeting and continued their household chores. Therefore, women's increased participation in the public sphere did not necessarily indicate that women's position within the households had improved.

The formation of women's groups was considered a significant change in the communities. Group formation meant that women had become active, took part in meetings and asked questions. In a meeting of a dairy-user group in a hill village in western Nepal, about 15 men and 8 women were participating in the dairy committee monthly meeting. Collectively, the women (who sat together) were vocal in the meeting and questioned the decisions made by the core-group dominated by men. After their meeting, we asked the women what they thought about the women's situation in their village. Before the women could reply, a man answered the question, saying that discrimination against women had decreased in recent years. He said, 'Women are no longer discriminated against; these days women have got rights. Things have changed considerably.' A woman reacted angrily to his comments, 'How can you say so? How do you know? You can't say anything just like that; you should ask us … What do you know about us?' Following this, all the other women present echoed her words. Women's participation in the public sphere has strengthened their confidence to raise their voice and ask questions.

Informants said that, previously, women's representation was minimal and almost non-existent. In the last 10 to 15 years, women were increasingly represented in local committees and decision-making structures at the local level, that is, representation in VDC, user groups, health post advisory committees and school governing boards. Participation in these activities had resulted in some women's agency increasing considerably. There was increased leadership of women in the village-level formal institutions. Several women were seen travelling out of their villages to take part in the meetings organised by NGOs on the issues of women's empowerment, forestry, saving and credit, among others.

Despite impressive changes in women's participation and representation in various public activities, traditional roles in terms of household chores had not transformed. One young married woman in a hill village in western Nepal commented, 'The only change is that we have been told that we too have rights. In our daily life, we continue to cook, look after children and wash.' She added, 'We talk about equality, but men's attitude has not changed. My neighbour picks his wife's petticoat (drying in the sun) using sticks, but not using his hands.' It was almost impossible for us to organise interviews and group discussions with women in the evenings. Men would say that women would not be able to come to meetings, as it was time for them to cook. Public places like village tea shops were still occupied by men only.

In a hill village in western Nepal, a group of women was meeting in the yard of a village house. When asked what had changed in their lives, they said that they were still poor, but now they were 'aware'. When asked to give examples of what that meant practically, one woman jokingly said, 'It means that if my husband beats me, I know I have the right to beat him back!' Reacting to women's assertiveness in the public sphere, a middle-aged man said, 'Women used to cover their heads with *ghungat* (a cover), but now women wear revealing clothes showing their navels. They react aggressively when men tease them.'

Several women, who openly supported the Maoists, said that the Maoist movement had challenged gender-based discrimination significantly. A young married woman in a hill village in western Nepal, who was otherwise critical of the Maoists, opined that some of the Maoist actions had given more confidence to women. She said, 'Many women now walk around with AK-47. We have to remember that, previously, they were not allowed to go out of their homes. This leads to a "mental change".' This view was not always shared by others for whom there was no connection between women's empowerment and the Maoist movement. To them, the Maoists had done nothing apart from recruiting Maoists to fight and punishing a few men for drinking and playing cards.

Radio programmes (particularly FM radio) played an important role in raising public awareness on the issue. Similarly, a few informants felt that many young men and women who went to the cities for further education and employment opportunities brought ideas of women's rights to their villages. Increasingly, the debate on women's backwardness had formed a regular discussion topic in tea shops (among men) and at water taps (among women).

There was a widespread perception among men and women that women's lives have changed considerably in the last 15 years. This included, among other points, increased confidence among women, awareness of their rights, increased freedom to participate in community activities, increased decision-making power, improved health, increased labour participation and reduced incidents of domestic violence.

The Shift in Local Power Relations

There has been a major change in terms of the material aspects of labour relations with a clear shift from caste-based or other forms of attached labour to cash-based wage labour both within and outside agriculture, but also in the more symbolic aspects of labour relations in terms of the awareness of labourers' identity as citizens with rights. Broadly speaking, there was a recognition that semi-feudal or caste-based attachment to labour was 'exploitative' and increasing opportunities for wage labour both within and outside the village had opened up significant opportunities to transcend such attachment. Traditionally, labourers have been conceived as subjects, both by the state and by their owners/employers. The dominant class, especially the upper caste and those who owned land, had control over the poorer households. According to Regmi (1978), since the 19th century in rural Nepal, the mukhiya and zamindar were not just landowners, but also representatives of the central government who collected revenue and performed various judicial and administrative functions. The state was able to impose a labour tax as well as extract free labour from the peasants. Therefore, these forced systems did not allow the peasant to make any economic gains, as there was no return for these services; on the contrary, 'it allowed the state to exercise authority over the peasant not only as a tenant but also as a subject' (Regmi 1978, 104).

Over the last decades, various political and socio-economic transformations have played a significant role in challenging feudal relations in rural Nepal. These changes have meant that labourers and labouring households embedded in traditional caste-based practices, who saw themselves as subjects without rights, are now asserting themselves as conscious political and economic agents and are increasingly seen by others as such. This consciousness was strongly driven by the discourses of rights and empowerment as advocated by many of the NGOs and local groups working in the villages, as well as the Maoists. Hence, traditional semi-feudal labouring practices have been challenged, and labourers and labouring households are now asserting their rights through new politicised identities such as Kamaiyas, Haliyas or Dalits. Fujikura (2004), in a study of the Kamaiya freedom movement in the western Terai, looks at the effect of these discourses. He explains that the freedom movement of the Kamaiyas led by BASE (grassroots organisation) was an outcome of the history of development interventions in the region. There are several cases showing these identity formations taking place. A Dalit man in a hill village in western Nepal worked as *hali* (bonded tiller) for the Bahuns and Magars of the village. He also worked as a *katwal* (messenger) for about 30–35 years. An episode of resistance against the low wages by some of the occupational workers resulted in him losing his job. However, the resistance meant that he was able to come out of the patron-client relation. A Tharu man in a Terai village had worked as a *haruwa* (bonded labourer) for the local landlord for about 33 years. When the Maoists came to power, he was freed. After being freed of the *haruwa* bond, he began to work for the landlord in *adhiya* (sharecropping). This meant that he had more time for himself and was free to seek other labour work. Similarly, according to a man in a hill village in western Nepal, 'In the Panchayat system, labourers like me had to work as *hali* for the upper-caste people and had to work free of cost. But things have reasonably changed after the multiparty democracy, because people like me have become aware and without any fear can speak out for our rights and existence. Earlier, we could hardly participate in any sort of gathering, but now we can participate in different programmes and have become much cleverer than before.' Another way in which this transformation is established for the Kamaiya is by having an identity card or being registered in the local land reform office with land certificates. Identity cards were very important for people to establish themselves as freed Kamaiyas. According to a Tharu man in a village in western Terai, 'If I have an identification card, then I can fight for my rights.' By forming various groups with the support of NGOs, the Kamaiyas have been able to raise their problems with state officials.

Various groups and committees established in rural areas have been advocating for the rights of the poor. A president of a local Haliya group in a hill village in western Nepal explained that his group had been working to disseminate information about the problems of poor Haliyas, conducting awareness classes and training the poor on standing up for their rights and privileges. In the Terai, the term 'kamaiya' was traditionally used to denote the labour relationship between the landlord and bonded labour, but has now been formally recognised as an identity of landless people by the state. With these new identities, various groups have been demanding rights and entitlements from the state and other organisations. Therefore, the labouring classes have gradually turned from being landlords' subjects to state citizens and are able to articulate their demands and rights better. While there is a transition of the labourers' position from subjects to citizens associated with changing labour relations and wider socio-economic and political changes in Nepal, this transition is not a linear one from unfreedom to freedom.

As I discuss in the next chapter, most labouring households must rely on both agriculture and non-agricultural labour as one works as an insurance against the other. It has become almost impossible for labouring households to sustain themselves exclusively either on agriculture or on non-land-based wage work and, therefore, must draw their livelihoods from both. Despite the increase in migration and wage labour, the village often continues to be the key unit for the organisation of labour, particularly for women workers who are stuck with housework and children, and for those with very little financial or social capital.

'Previously, zamindars ruled. We had to consult them for everything (looks towards his father for approval). Now we can do what we want; isn't it? Now they have left; you can go and see their house; it's all reduced to rubble.' This young man in a village in western Nepal was referring to three landlords, who owned over 50 *bigha*[3] of land, and who had left the village following the conflict. When asked what had happened to their property, including the land, he replied, 'Their relatives are looking after the house, landless people cultivate some land ... I don't know what will happen now. I hear that the land will be returned to them.' What his young man shared largely reflects the situation of landlords and captured land in the aftermath of the Maoist insurgency in rural Nepal. While this landlord's fate is unknown, many landlords were able to re-secure their land, following the Comprehensive Peace Agreement.

There was a common perception that the landlords and other upper-class people had lost some of their authority during the conflict period. Following the Maoist insurgency, most landed-class people had left the village (voluntarily or by force) and relocated to nearby towns or Kathmandu. In the areas where Maoists had a strong presence, several landlords had completely abandoned their property, while, in other areas, landed and upper-class people had left their property to someone they trusted in the village (usually a relative) and became absentee landlords. After joining mainstream politics, the Maoists had begun to return land that belonged to landlords in areas where their influence was less strong. In this sense, there was no long-term effect on land distribution as a result of the Maoists capturing property/land. However, the situation in Maoist strongholds was different: a significant number of Maoists (and those

3 1 *bigha* equals 8,316.8 square metres.

calling themselves 'free Kamaiyas') had captured land belonging to absentee landlords and, more recently, forest land belonging to the state, and were still holding on to it.

With the growth of the Maoists' influence, landholding had become a problem for the landowning class. Landowners perceived that the Maoist government would either take their property away or significantly reduce the land area. As a result, the landowners were making every effort to sell their agricultural land or reduce the size of their holdings. It was the households with migrant remittances from the Gulf States or Malaysia (and to some extent from India), who bought land from landowners. There was a clear sign of land fragmentation as a result of remittance flow into the villages. This process enabled the landowning households to buy small pieces of land in the nearby cities or Kathmandu, sell the village land and eventually relocate.

More critically, as we shall discuss in the next chapter, growth of the non-farm economy in rural areas meant that land was not always an important marker of class in the villages; rather, it was the money (mostly gained through remittances and wage labour), a secure job and education, which was increasingly considered an important symbol of status in the villages. Schooling and education were perceived as the most important routes to social mobility, though young men and women were aware that schooling and education did not automatically mean social mobility. The opening of roads and market access had facilitated improvement in the economic situation of a few households. As a result, some peasant households had turned entrepreneurs (for example, selling milk, vegetables, fruits and other products in local markets), successfully improving their socio-economic situation. To some extent, this process undermined the traditional authority of the landowning class. Similarly, the growth of absentee landlords in the villages meant that poorer households did not have to live under the constant interaction with and traditional authority of the landlords.

Nature and Drivers of Social Transformation

From the above, we can see that the two most important forms of social change are: 'increased awareness and education' and 'increased collective agency of discriminated groups'. People repeatedly emphasised that 'they had become aware' and their 'sense of confidence and self-esteem had increased considerably'. People had gone through an internal transformation process from 'not knowing' to 'knowing' and from 'lack of confidence' to 'increased collective agency to raise their concerns and rights'. Perhaps the most important 'step-change' was seen in the caste domain where there has been a significant reduction in discriminatory practices, more evident in the public than in the private sphere and the increased agency of Dalits. Women's collective agency had equally increased. Alongside the politicisation of ethnicity at the centre, there was a sense that local people were increasingly aware of their ethnic identity and had begun to take part in various ethnic mobilisations at the local level. Interestingly, the Maoist insurgency and the Kamaiyas' movement have brought the issue of class and land distribution to the forefront.

Although the Maoist insurgency, at its core, raised the issues of rights, recognition, discrimination and state and development failure, there was no causal relationship between the Maoist insurgency and transformation in rural Nepal. In some ways, the Maoists were viewed as an accelerator of change, an important vector of transformation. But they were not the only one.

What then were the drivers of change? The Maoists played an important role in two ways. Firstly, the Maoists' political agenda and slogans provided a political space required for the emergence and sustenance of a transformative process in Nepali society. This was useful to place the issues of recognition, voice and representation in the political and administrative structure on the political agenda and get political legitimacy for transformation. Secondly, at the local level, Maoist tactics of social transformation were seen to be more reactive than proactive, that is, generally, Maoist activists did not take a proactive role in challenging discrimination/mobilising oppressed groups. However, they did play a reactive role, that is, they were quick to react when cases of discrimination were reported locally. Their usual method was to punish the 'culprit'. They focused on 'culprits' rather than on 'victims'. In addition, the Maoists carried out a range of political activities, in the form of various messages, public speeches, village theatres or cultural programmes in some areas of Nepal, aimed at promoting the agency of Dalits, women, landless peasants and other marginalised groups.

Although NGOs and CBOs sometimes competed around the same agenda of discrimination and rights, the role of NGOs and CBOs in promoting social change was different from that of the Maoists. Their approach was based on social mobilisation, community organisation and educating local people using Freirian models of conscientisation and empowerment. The approach was group-based and proactive rather than reactive, that is, NGOs focused on working directly with the marginalised and oppressed groups and not with the institutions, individuals or groups responsible for the discrimination. Given the widespread focus on public advocacy, NGOs and human rights organisations did not have effective ways to address access to justice for victims of violence and discrimination. Thus, the individual cases of violence, ill-treatment and discrimination that remained undocumented, and therefore unaddressed, resulted in the absence of justice for the victims and a cycle of impunity.

Overall, the occupation of political space at the macro level (created mainly by the Maoists) and local social space (largely created by the NGOs and CBOs and to some extent by the Maoists) together seem to have been instrumental in bringing about the perceptions of transformation. With the radical restructuring of the Nepali state, there is no 'going back' on issues of awareness of rights and the more symbolic aspects of caste or gender discrimination. What emerges nonetheless is an interesting relationship between education,

Maoist insurgency and the role of NGOs in bringing about symbolic transformation. The relationship between the Maoist insurgency that led to the displacement of upper-caste landlords, lack of growth in land prices in rural areas and the perceived threat of a limit on the size of land holding, made it possible for remittance-receiving households to buy land.

Concluding Discussion

The Maoist insurgency seems to have functioned as an accelerator of change, certainly in terms of 'awareness' of issues of structural violence and justice, which is attributed to the Maoists and, to some extent, to the work of development actors and NGOs. These issues of social justice are now clearly to the forefront of people's minds. This is expressed in many ways—including the denial by high-caste people that there is any discrimination based on caste and, conversely, in the emergent perception among the upper castes that they are beginning to suffer from reverse discrimination.

Similarly, some of the upper-caste old guards are finding it difficult to transition to a situation where the rights of former subjects clash with their perception of their past inherited authority. Upper-caste assertion has been visible in the form of violence against Dalits, women and landless people. Increased cases of sexual violence against Dalit girls and women in recent years point to such resistance and backlash.

In summary, the seeds of social change were sown before the insurgency, primarily due to livelihood diversification, outmigration, the flow of remittances, roads, schooling, the presence of development programmes and ideas of modernity and development. Awareness-raising had also started much before the insurgency. The process of change in Nepal, as everywhere, is dictated by context, confusing, uneven and fraught with backlashes. The evidence from Nepal shows that transformation in caste, gender and local power relations is more about the symbolic and 'awareness' aspects of social relationships. The call for equality, citizenship and rights is not necessarily met in reality.

References

Aahuti. 2010. *Nepalma Varnavyavastha ra Barga-Sangharsha*. Lalitpur: Samata Foundation.

Baral, L.R. 1977. *Oppositional Politics in Nepal*. New Delhi: Abhinav.

Bista, D.B. 1991. *Fatalism and Development: Nepal's Struggle for Modernization*. Calcutta: Orient Longman.

Blaikie, P, J. Cameron, and D. Seddon. 1980. *Nepal in Crisis: Growth and Stagnation at the Periphery*. Delhi: Oxford University Press.

Blaikie, P, J. Cameron, and D. Seddon. 2002. 'Understanding 20 Years of Change in West-Central Nepal: Continuity and Change in Lives and Ideas'. *World Development*, 30(7): 1255–1270.

Bohara, A. 2002. 'An End to the Means'. *Nepali Times*, 107 (16–22 August 2002). Available at: http://archive.nepalitimes.com/news.php?id=5792#.X3WCvtZ7k1i (Accessed on 20 September 2020).

DFID / World Bank. 2006. *Unequal Citizens: Gender, Caste and Ethnic Exclusion in Nepal*. Kathmandu: DFID / World Bank.

Dixit, K.M. 2009. *Dekheko Muluk*. Lalitpur: Jagadamba Prakashan.

Donini, A. and J. R. Sharma. 2008. *Humanitarian Agenda 2015: Nepal Case Study*. Medford, MA: Feinstein International Center, Tufts University.

Fujikura, T. 2004. *Discourses of Awareness: Development, Social Movements and Practices of Freedom in Nepal*. Department of Anthropology. PhD Dissertation, Illinois: University of Chicago.

Gautam, B., ed. 2008. *Madhes Bidrohako Nalibeli*. Kathmandu, Nepal: Martin Chautari.

Gellner, D.N. 2007. 'Caste, Ethnicity, and Inequality in Nepal'. *Economic and Political Weekly*, 42(20): 1823–1828.

Gellner, D.N. 2007. 'Introduction: Transformation of the Nepalese State'. In *Resistance and the State: Nepalese Experiences*, edited by D.N. Gellner, 1–30. Oxford, New York: Berghahn Books.

Gellner, D.N., J. Pfaff-Czarnecka, and J. Whelpton, eds. 1997. *Nationalism and Ethnicity in a Hindu Kingdom*. Netherlands: Harwood Academic Publishers.

Gersony, R. 2003. *Sowing the Wind...: History and Dynamics of the Maoist Revolt in Nepal's Rapti Hills*. Portland, Oregon: Mercy Corps International.

Government of Nepal and Communist Party of Nepal (Maoist). 2006. *Comprehensive Peace Agreement*. Kathmandu: Government of Nepal.

Guneratne, A. 1998. 'Modernization, the State, and the Construction of a Tharu Identity in Nepal'. *The Journal of Asian Studies*, 57(3): 749–773.

Gurung, H. 1997. 'State and Society in Nepal'. In *Nationalism and Ethnicity in a Hindu Kingdom*, edited by D.N. Gellner et al., 495–532. Amsterdam: Harwood Academic Publishers.

Gyawali, B. 2018. *Ambiguous Bikās: History of the Concept of Development in Nepal 1900–2006*, PhD thesis. Finland: Department of Political and Economic Studies, University of Helsinki.

Hachethu, K. 2009. 'The Communist Party of Nepal (Maoist): Transformation from an Insurgency Group to a Competitive Political Party'. *European Bulletin for Himalayan Research*, 33–34: 39–72.

Hagen, S. L. 2010. *The Rise of Ethnic Politics in Nepal: Democracy in the Margins*. London: Routledge.

Hutt, M., ed. 2004. *Himalayan People's War: Nepal's Maoist Rebellion*. London: Hurst & Company.

ICG. 2007. *Nepal's Troubled Tarai Region*. 136/Asia. Nepal: International Crisis Group. Available at: https://www.crisisgroup.org/asia/south-asia/nepal/nepal-s-troubled-tarai-region (Accessed on 20 September 2020).

Jha, P. 2014. *Battles of the New Republic: A Contemporary History of Nepal*. London: C Hurst & Co.

Justice, J. 1986. *Policies, Plans and People: Foreign Aid and Health Development*. Berkeley: University of California Press.

Lawoti, M. 2005. *Towards a Democratic Nepal: Inclusive Political Institutions for a Multicultural Society*. New Delhi and London: Sage Publications.

Martin, I. 2012. 'The United Nations and Support to Nepal's Peace Process: The Role of the UN Mission in Nepal'. In *Nepal in Transition from People's War to Fragile Peace*, edited by S. von Einsiedel, M.D. Malone, and S. Pradhan, 201–231. Cambridge: Cambridge University Press.

Mikesell, S. 1993. *The Paradoxical Support of Nepal's Left for Comrade Gonzalo*. Kathmandu: Himal Books, 31–33 (April/May).

Nickson, A. 1992. 'Democratisation and the Growth of Communism in Nepal: A Peruvian Scenario in the Making?'. *The Journal of Commonwealth & Comparative Politics*, 30(3): 358–386.

Ogura, K. 2008. 'Maoist People's Governments, 2001–2005: The Power in Wartime'. In *Local Democracy in South Asia: Microprocesses of Democratization in Nepal and Its Neighbours*, edited by D.N. Geller and K. Hachethu, 175–231. Delhi: Sage.

Onta, P. 2002: 'Critiquing the Media Boom'. In *State of Nepal*, edited by K.N. Dixit and S. Ramachandran, 253–269. Kathmandu: Himal Books.

Onta, P. 2006. 'The Growth of the Adivasi and Janajati Movement in Nepal after 1990: The Non-Political Institutional Agents'. *Studies in Nepali History and Society*, 11(2): 303–354.

Pfaff-Czarnecka, J. 1997. 'Vestiges and Visions: Cultural Change in the Process of Nation- Building in Nepal'. In *Nationalism and Ethnicity in a Hindu Kingdom*, edited by D.N. Gellner et al., 419–470. Amsterdam: Harwood Academic Publishers.

Pradhan, R. 2005. *The Ain of 1854 and after: Legal Pluralism, Models of Society and Ethnicity in Nepal*, Paper presented at the conference 'Negotiating Ethnicity in Nepal's Past and Present', Kathmandu.

Rai, K. 2020. '"Nepali" versus "Nepalka Mahila": Mahila Aandolanharu ra Bididhata'. *Samaj Adhyayan*, 15: 9–32.

Rai, O.A. 2016. 'What was it all for?'. *Nepali Times*, 794. Available at: https://archive.nepalitimes.com/article/nation/revisiting-maoist-demands,2860 (Accessed on 20 September 2020).

Regmi, M.C. 1978. *Thatched Huts and Stucco Palaces: Peasants and Landlords in the 19th Century Nepal*. New Delhi: Vikas.

Robertson, T.B. 2018. 'DDT and the Cold War Jungle: American Environmental and Social Engineering in the Rapti Valley of Nepal'. *Journal of American History*, 104(4): 904–930.

Sharma, J.R. 2012. 'Social Science Engagement and Political Interregnum in Nepal'. *Economic and Political Weekly*, 47(31): 45–48.

Sharma, S. 2019. *Nepal Nexus*. New Delhi: Penguin Books.

Shneiderman, S. and M. Turin 2004. 'The Path to Janasarkar in Dolakha District: Towards an Ethnography of the Maoist Movement'. In *Himalayan People's War: Nepal's Maoist Rebellion*, edited by M. Hutt, 77–109. London: Hurst & Co.

Subedi, M. 2014. 'Afno Manchhe: Unequal Access to Public Resources and Institutions in Nepal'. Dhaulagiri Journal of Sociology and Anthropology, 8: 55–86.

Sunam, R. 2018. *Sambeshitako Bahas*. Lalitpur: Samata Foundation.

Thapa, D. 2019. 'Negotiating a "New Nepal": Evolving Relationship between Inclusion and Peace'. In *Negotiating Inclusion in Peace Processes*, edited by Andy Carl, 61–66. Accord 28, Conciliation Resources, 2019.

Whelpton, J. 2005. *History of Nepal*. Cambridge: Cambridge University Press.

Women carrying large basket of fodder, Rolpa, 2009.

3

Peasantry, Mobility and the Changing Face of Rural Nepal

Introduction

'If I had received vegetable farming training before, I would not have migrated to Lebanon,' said Sushila Tamang, vegetable farmer and former migrant domestic worker.[1]

'Meet Lal Bahadur Kadal. He was thinking of migrating to India for work like most of his fellow villagers have done. But, instead, through our support, he participated in seed production training and received vegetable seeds. He then organised himself and 11 other local farmers into a Seed Producer Group. With our further support, the group was introduced to seed traders throughout the country.

In their first year of operation, the group produced and sold around 1 metric tonne (mt) of seed. This increased to 7 mt the year after and, in 2005, the group was contracted to produce 14 mt. The number of seed growers in the village has increased too; there are now 175 members in the group.

Lal Bahadur earned almost £1,000 from selling radish seed this year, 8 times higher than Nepal's per capita income.'[2]

'Case studies' like those quoted above, appearing in glossy reports and websites of development agencies, reflect a view of agriculture as a regular part of rural livelihoods in the Global

1 Source: https://www.ilo.org/infostories/en-GB/Stories/Country-Focus/nepal (Accessed on September 2020).

2 Source: http://www.dfid.gov.uk/casestudies/files/asia/nepal-seeds.asp (Accessed on 15 May 2005).

South, where outmigration is seen as an aberrant feature of rural society. Accordingly, rural and agricultural development projects are conceptualised, designed and implemented to stop people from migrating and keeping them in their home locality (Sharma 2008). For most scholars and development practitioners, it is given that Nepal is seen as an agrarian society, where land is a critical source of livelihood. Reflecting this view, much of the development interventions since the 1950s have focused on agricultural development and land reform. Over the last several decades, we have been told repeatedly that agriculture is the most important source of livelihood for 80–90 per cent of Nepalis. While development policies were framed differently under different development and political regimes, a uniform voice came from policy documents that agriculture must be the central element in any strategy for economic development in Nepal. While there is no disagreement on agriculture as one of the central elements in the livelihoods of Nepalis, it remains surprising to see that even those who do not own land or do not derive their subsistence from farming are automatically categorised as farmers or *kisan* or *krishak* in policy discourses.

Reflecting on the regular practice of outmigration from far-western Nepal and its implications for rural development, Pfaff-Czarnecka makes the following observation:

> Migrants are farmers and of course, members of rural households and of rural communities, but as 'migrants' they are absent from a given local rural context. They have become a part of the urban labour force. Hence, from the perspective of outside observers, it is difficult to think of them as constituent agents of 'rural development'. Still, the temporary absence of the migrants from the local economies and from the local socio-political contexts, and their continuous movement between home and 'outside', is a crucial factor affecting contemporary life within marginal rural areas. (Pfaff-Czarnecka 1995, 97)

While there is no denying that land and agriculture have historically been the most important source of power in rural Nepal and their legacy in shaping economic and political power structures continues, they do not have the same status today. These days, power emanates from other variables, such as access to education, cash income from remittances, control over development funds and social and political networks among others.

Such sedentary representations of the Nepali peasantry appear partial and inconsistent when compared with historical and ethnographic evidence on the widespread culture of migration. Not only does such a sedentary view disregard the ubiquitous presence, normalcy and importance of mobility, it completely misses the historic transformation underway in Nepal in terms of mobility of labour and changed moral economies of subsistence agriculture in a once-remote village. Such views do not allow us to understand transformations underway in rural Nepal, where migrant labour from the village has disrupted moral economic institutions and norms, and their sociocultural consequences.

Ethnographic evidence shows that one of the significant transformations in rural Nepal's political economy is the gradual weakening of traditional forms of attached and caste-based division of labour alongside widespread labour mobility. Not only has there been a diversification of rural livelihoods from land- and agriculture-based to non-agricultural and non-land-based sources, there is also a growing and widespread mobility of labour within and outside the country, resulting in what I have called 'culture of migration' (Sharma 2019). Mobility ranges from commuting for day labour to nearby areas and seasonal mobility to towns and cities within the country or across the border to India, to the organised migration to global destinations such as the Gulf, Southeast Asia and beyond.

A Brief Economic and Social History of Peasantry in Nepal

Compared to widespread writing on Nepal's political history, there is limited literature on the social history (Onta 1994). There is historical evidence of unequal and exploitative socio-economic relations of production and extractive state policies that have created conditions for impoverishment of the peasantry (Regmi 1976, Regmi 1978, Shrestha 2001, Blaikie et al. 2002). According to Blaikie et al. (2002), the major role of the peasantry in the political economy of Nepal, since the formation of a tributary state in the late 18th century, has been to provide a surplus to the ruling aristocracy. They further explain that 'the economy of the peasant is essentially a domestic one in which production is for the use of household or kin, and surpluses, such as they exist, are redistributed by payments to the temple, festivals, poor relatives, etc.' (Blaikie et al. 2002, 64). The destitution of the peasantry was maintained through three key inter related domains of power: unequal distribution of land, use of forced labour and extraction of rent (Regmi 1976).

First, the land has remained a major source of status, power, prosperity and subsistence in Nepal (Regmi 1976). In this context, it was only natural that those who had more land commanded greater economic and political power. Historically, the land has been appropriated by different elite groups, most notably by dominant castes, through different landholding systems. Those who were not related to the ruling elite or their patronage networks were excluded from land ownership, which impacted their socio-economic and political position for many centuries.

Broadly speaking, landholding in the country involved four main systems (Regmi 1976, Regmi 1961), and this does not include the *kipat* system found in eastern Nepal (Caplan 1990). First is *raikar* land, which is owned by the state but given to people, mostly those from higher castes, to cultivate and pay dues for the privilege.

The tenants had no rights over the land. The second was *birta* land, given by the rulers to their loyal patrons, priests, soldiers and the royal family, who in turn sub-let to tenants. The key element of *birta* land was that the landlords did not have to pay tax, which is considered the key factor causing landlordism in Nepal. The third system is *jagir*, which refers to land assigned to government employees as a payment for their services. The fourth was *guthi* land. Under the *guthi* system, land grants or endowments were made to charitable, religious or philanthropic institutions. These four forms of land tenure have shaped the element of privilege and precarity in Nepal's agrarian structure. Largely, powerless, landless people depended on rural landowners for their livelihood, often working as tenants, sharecroppers or domestic workers (Regmi 1976, Shrestha 2001). As such, poor peasants' interaction with the land was mostly mediated through their land tenancy and sharecropping (Shrestha 2008).

Despite political integration through the unification process led by Prithvi Narayan Shah, Nepal's economic integration was never achieved, and this was reflected in different types of land tenure patterns influenced by British, Mughal and Hindu systems coexisting with the Nepalese system (Regmi 1961). Historically and legally, Nepal's land tenure system was characterised by state ownership, landlordism and limited peasants' rights. Although there have been attempts at land reform, especially post-1950, the changes have been limited, and the effects of the age-old system still directly impact the distribution of political and economic power in Nepal.

Under these systems, land distribution was unequal and based on loyalty and caste-based patronage networks, which benefited high castes and people with networks in the ruling class, marginalising those already impoverished. Those close to the ruling elite were able to accumulate and own land through land grants from the rulers, which resulted in a landed class. High-caste landlords, living mostly in cities, employed local peasants to cultivate their land and extracted more rent than was invested back (Regmi 1961). This provided the landowning elite with plenty of surplus, thus, reinforcing class inequalities. However, according to Regmi, these taxes and rents did not supplement the state revenue, nor were they reinvested in agricultural development. Hence, Regmi concludes that the reason for Nepal's continued existence as a poor country during the 19th century was because of 'low productivity due to inadequate capital investment in agriculture' which forced the rural peasants to live in poverty (Regmi 1978, 179).

In addition, the Shah and Rana rulers extensively recruited and benefitted from the recruitment of labour for their territorial expansion of the Gorkha empire and during various episodes of war (Regmi 1988). Poor peasants were mobilised not only to engage in the battlefield, but also to serve as porters to help transport goods, weapons and other supplies. Labour was also forcibly recruited to build roads, temples, palaces and other buildings for the ruling class, and this was unpaid. The ruling elite was able to impose labour tax and extract free labour from the peasants. Various forced and bonded labour systems continued, which gave the peasants no benefits as there was no just return for their services. The ruling elite, often based on caste and patronage networks, made excessive use of unpaid labour. Peasant children worked in homes, farms or mines, and the practice has continued in modern days. Despite abolition, various forms of forced and bonded labour have continued. There was a widespread practice of compulsory labour by the state until 1950 in the northern regions of Kathmandu, inhabited by Tamangs subjected to mandatory labour practices mainly for butter, fruit, paper production and porterage. Villagers had to manage their subsistence within a system where there were no limitations to such labour obligations (Holmberg and March 1999). Ill treatment and exploitation of peasants and their families contributed to their protracted precarity (Raj 2010).

Moreover, as indicated above, peasants were subjected to hardship from additional exploitation through the extraction of tax by local administrations, temples and state officials. Regmi (1978) explores the agrarian tax system in 19th-century Nepal, in which mandatory payments had to be made in cash or kind to the local elite, landowners and the government by the peasants. Explaining the various systems of tax collection instituted by the state to extract labour from the peasants to generate a steady flow of income to the landowning elites and generate government, he writes, 'The system left the peasants at a minimum level of subsistence, and took little account of the need to reinvest a portion of the agricultural surplus to raise the standard of living of the peasant' (Regmi 1978, 74).

Such harsh economic conditions meant that many peasant families were forced to out-migrate in search of labouring jobs (Shrestha 2001). These exploitative state policies had a lasting impact on peasant livelihoods and survival, prompting them to escape the suffering to seek work opportunities elsewhere, including outside the political boundary of Nepal. As early as the 1850s, Nepali men facing economic insecurities began to travel across the border to Sikkim, Assam, Darjeeling, Bhutan and Burma (now Myanmar), looking for work in coal factories. They were also employed as porters, and as tea plantation, domestic and construction workers, among other occupations. The recruitment in the British Army, that formally started after 1816, did offer employment opportunities for men from certain hill ethnic groups, although they would be engaged in life-threatening and dangerous work while being away from their families and farms.

Changing Rural Society

Nepali villages have recently undergone significant changes. With the construction of road networks, increased budget flows for development activities, growth of market areas, mobile phone networks, widespread mobility and flow of remittances, Nepali villages look increasingly different from the way they did a few decades ago. Rural livelihoods are intrinsically connected to cities and towns (Mishra 2010). Land and agriculture no longer remain the only source of livelihoods. There has been a general decline in agriculture in remote rural areas, due to the exodus of labour into non-land-based livelihood activities and a general perception of the declining value of agricultural work. The integration of rural societies into national and global economic and political flows are disrupting livelihood patterns and the socio-cultural fabric in remote locations (Mishra 2010, Campbell 2018, Sharma 2019).

Longitudinal studies conducted in the hills of Nepal have indicated the profound impact of outmigration in rural villages. Blaikie et al. (2002) concluded from their empirical research that the only social change in the previous 20 years in rural western Nepal was the 'degree of continuity' towards deepening poverty. They found that there had been very little change in the rural class structure, and concluded that there had been no significant changes in the development of commercialised agriculture, in the cost of hired labour and no improvement in livelihoods. Yet, they noticed changes in the semi-feudal system, including how outmigration and urban growth, which had been underestimated in their previous study (Blaikie et al. 1980), had resulted in significant alterations in labour relations and livelihoods. This important trend has the potential to effect significant change in rural class structure, which the authors underestimated. Ben Campbell's longitudinal study in a Tamang village in northern Nepal documents a notable transition in village livelihoods from an agrarian to a remittance economy supported by temporary labour migration. He then offers some intriguing social gaps and sociocultural consequences of outmigration in the village life (Campbell 2018). Reflecting on 30 years of change in a Gurung village north of Pokhara, Alan Macfarlane found that the importance of migrant remittances from the army and civilian work, as described in his original study (Macfarlane 1976), had declined, with remittances reduced to a trickle from the few labourers abroad, who saved a little and sent it home. From the middle of the 1970s, when army recruitment dried up, village men went first to India and later to East and Southeast Asia, the Middle East and a few to Europe and America. When these men and the remaining army servicemen retired, they no longer came back to the village, but settled in towns, particularly in nearby Pokhara. Further, Macfarlane argued that a key effect of this outmigration had been that those left behind bore the burden of the migration through material impoverishment (Macfarlane 2001). Another study by Jagannath Adhikari in a village in Kaski district shows how migrant remittances, which were the primary source of cash, had a dual impact on labour opportunities. During the early 1990s, remittances assisted 'marginal farmers' and 'landless labourers' in their livelihoods 'through the creation of land-renting and labour employment opportunities within the villages' (Adhikari 2001, 248–249). Remittance-receiving village households invested the cash in agriculture and were able to employ agricultural labourers to work on the farm. However, towards the end of the 1990s, there was a trend towards migrant households investing the remittances in land, housing and businesses in urban areas. There was a gradual decline in investment in rural agriculture and shrinking work opportunities for labouring households. This led to a further escalation of rural to urban migration, especially from poor and disadvantaged communities (Adhikari 2001). Other studies have found that about half of rural households have at least one overseas migrant at any given point (Sunam 2014, Adhikari and Hobley 2015). The widespread prevalence of migration and its impact on Nepal's remittance economy has been documented and acknowledged in recent years (Seddon et al. 2002).

Several studies have looked at the impact of the cash economy in rural Nepal. Anthropologist John Hitchcock conducted a study in the hills of central Nepal in a Magar village in the late 1950s that concluded that income from working for the Indian or the British Army in India was the main way to cope with the increased monetisation and improve the economic status of many in the village (Hitchcock 1961). With the increase in the availability of goods in nearby markets, there was also an increase in cash demand. The salaries of soldiers and, more importantly, their pensions became the primary sources of cash for many households. This also created an increase in the money-lending processes in the villages. Reflecting on the cash flow in the village, Hitchcock concluded that households connected with the army were able to improve their economic status, while the others were having difficulty coping with the increased cash requirements. Similarly, Panter-Brick and Eggerman (1997) found that migration to the lowlands of Nepal or the cities in India for employment were coping strategies for households with low agriculture production and seasonal food deficit in western Nepal. Some migrant workers returned with substantial amounts of money and could make investments, whereas, some from poorer households only earned enough to support themselves. The study also found that, for some families, these coping strategies created opportunities for income and eventual possibilities for investment. However, for other families, especially those from poorer households, these strategies only led to 'greater debt, economic marginalisation, and impoverishment' (Panter-Brick and Eggerman 1997, 190).

Likewise, Patricia Caplan (1972) has looked at the changes in political and economic relations between high caste Brahmins and the Cobbler caste (untouchables) in a Hindu village in western Nepal post-1951. The growth of the market had affected the village economy, and there had been an increase in the need for cash in the village. While earlier cash was only available outside the village, the changes had brought cash into the village. Opportunities for employment and unskilled labour had benefitted both the Brahmins and the untouchables. However, these opportunities had different effects; Brahmins could use cash to lend at high-interest rates or invest in purchasing land. The Cobblers, on the other hand, spent their extra cash compensating for their greater grain deficit and were not able to use it to improve their living standards. The study concluded that although there existed an unequal distribution of wealth among

Brahmins and Cobblers, there had been changes in the economic relations between them. The new economic opportunities might not have improved the economic status of the untouchables, but had made them increasingly independent of the Brahmins, on whom they were previously dependent for cash and grains (Caplan 1972).

In another study, Lionel Caplan (1990) looked at the economic interdependence of Brahmins and Limbus in eastern Nepal. Cash raised by Limbus from wage labour, domestic service and petty trade had eased the burden of agricultural insufficiency and the need to rely on mortgages. However, this cash was not able to contribute positively to the overall economic situation of the Limbu households. The participation in the 'commercial' economy of the region had little impact on the economic dependence between the Limbus and the Brahmins. However, this relationship was affected by the employment of Limbus in the Army, as Limbus were able to acquire considerable cash income from sources outside agriculture, and they were able to invest this wealth in purchasing land, 'displacing Brahmins as landlords' (Caplan 1990, 108). Thus, agriculture no longer remained the primary source of income for the Limbus, and the income sources from the Army recruitment threatened the economic interdependence between these groups.

Other studies have looked into specific forms of bonded labour and their implications. Chhetri (2005) studied the social and economic problems of the Tharus from a historical perspective, and how the socio-economic and political environment contributed to their exploitation and oppression. Under the traditional Kamaiya system, landlords were dependent on the Kamaiya-Tharus to ensure a supply of labour. This dependence would provide a 'social safety net' for both the groups with possibilities for a Kamaiya farmer to be transformed into an 'independent' farmer. However, the expansion of the state into the Terai in the 19th century and the granting of land to Pahadis (people of hill origin) resulted in the separation of the Tharus from their farms. The appointment of migrant Pahadis for administering taxation and resettlement policies created a powerful new class in the Terai. This new landed class engaged the kamaiyas as bonded labourers. Chhetri explains that, under this system of bonded labour, the kamaiyas were contracted to the landlord for work, for which the family would receive a share of the production or payments made in kind. Under this contracting mechanism of labour and credit, it was impossible for the illiterate kamaiyas to free themselves, as they could not pay back the loans, which would eventually get larger. This form of bonded labour was prevalent in many Terai districts until it was officially abolished in 2000. However, Chettri argues that the haphazard process of freeing the kamaiyas has only resulted in them being forced to return to their landlords, migrate for work to India or starve due to unemployment as the state could not keep its promises of land and better livelihoods.

In his study of bonded labouring practices, Giri (2010) provides an insight into how the parents of working children and the landlords were utilising the promise of education as a safe meeting point and to transform traditional forms of agricultural bonded labour, like the Haliya and the Kamaiya systems. Although traditional practices had been denounced and, to some extent, banned, there was an increasing trend among families to send their children to work under a contract that offered education as a promise. However, this promise of education acted only as a 'magnet', as children were not allowed to attend a school or were engaged in so much work that they eventually dropped out of education. Hence, modern transformative forces like education did not necessarily bring changes in labour relations, as exploitative systems still existed, but in a different form than before.

In my previous work (Sharma 2019), I have outlined the following four themes on the changing face of rural Nepal.

Diversification of Rural Livelihoods

A key feature of livelihood diversification was a shift from land and agriculture to non-agriculture and non-land-based employment. In the past, people relied mainly on agriculture and traditional caste-based occupations for subsistence, with some income from outside in the form of remittances. However, in the last couple of decades, many households could hardly survive on agriculture or caste-based attached-labour for their subsistence. Many households depend on two, or more than two, sources for subsistence. Prominent sources of livelihood among the labourers are farming, including growing vegetables, wage labour (both within and outside the village), informal sector jobs in nearby markets or towns and migrant remittances. Despite livelihood diversification, people identify farming as their primary occupation. It was not important for households to depend on agriculture to identify as farmers. Farming provided a sense of identity, associated with rural dwelling, where people engaged in aspects of agriculture, although it played a less significant role in day-to-day living for many.

There is also a strong perception among young people that there is no benefit in agriculture and, with the expansion of education, young people are moving out of rural areas in search of work opportunities. According to a VDC secretary in a mid-western hill village, 'People in the village have the concept that educated people should not be doing agriculture, which was not productive, rather they should have a *jagir* (salaried job).'

A high-caste man in a hill village in western Nepal said that he could only grow 5 per cent of the paddy that his grandparents used to produce. He added, 'My sons have no other option than migrating to India for employment.' There have been shifts in the labour practices of poorer households. A Dalit man, who had worked as an agricultural labourer to pay off the interest on loans taken by his father, had recently stopped working for his high-caste landlord. He thought construction work was better than agricultural work, because 'it is easier and can be done with less hard work.' Construction work also provided him with more freedom, as he could choose when to work and when to stop working. The wages earned from construction work are 'very high', double the amount he earned as an agricultural labourer. A young Tharu man in a village in western Terai made wooden doors, cupboards and beds, in addition to his involvement in farming. Similarly, in a hill village in far western Nepal, besides farming and migration, men worked on the construction of school buildings, irrigation canals, private houses and trails within the village. Others temporarily migrated to India and worked as porters, or as labourers in stone quarries and road construction. The connection of rural areas to markets and cities through roads and communication has brought alternative livelihood sources for rural populations. This increase in market access has created new sources of wage labour and other opportunities in non-farm sectors. Men in far-western and mid-western villages come back from India during the plantation season and return for the harvest. Most peasant households had at least one family member, almost always male, working outside the country, mostly in India. A generation ago, most of these individuals were doing watchman jobs in India, but now some had started businesses, like running street food stalls in Indian cities. Tharu men, aged between 25 and 40 years, from Kamaiya families, were employed as daily wage labourers, unlike some of their fathers who were still working as Kamaiya. In the Terai districts in western Nepal, the freeing of the Kamaiya had created a shift in labour practices. Kamaiya households, who had previously worked for their landlords, had begun to work in various sectors of the economy after being 'freed'. While some continued to work as agricultural wage labourers, others had started working in the construction sector, migrated to India or taken up small service enterprises, such as plumbing, electric wiring, electronic goods repair shops, rickshaw pulling and cycle repairing, among others. These new skills were acquired through various training programmes provided by the government, NGOs and INGOs or offered in the market. Here, it is useful to highlight the gender dimensions of such a transition of labour from agriculture to non-agriculture and caste-based attached labour to wage labour. Most often, it is men who appear to be making this transition, with women still working in caste-based attached labour or agricultural labour. At the same time, increased outmigration of men has meant that the women who are left behind now work in the caste-based attached forms of agricultural labour. Overall, the findings indicate that livelihood diversification is a common practice. Remittances in many of the field sites have played an important role in securing the household subsistence. However, although people have seen an increased flow of money, labourers have not been able to increase their economic status sustainably.

The Weakening of Caste-Based Feudal Relations

Over the years, there has been a gradual weakening and disappearance of traditional labour arrangements, including the caste-based attached division of labour. Semi-feudal labour arrangements have been widespread in rural Nepal for many decades. Through the specific bonded systems of labour, such as Haliya or Kamaiya, and other caste-based occupations, many of the poorer households from lower castes relied on landlords or those with a better economic status for their subsistence. However, the expansion of the market and increased involvement of the state in development activities, party politics and, more recently, in the last decade, the Maoists' discourse on feudalism and the discourse of development and rights advocated by NGOs and various local groups have challenged the feudal system of labour arrangements. These developments have dented the status of those who had relied on the feudal system. A Dalit in a hill village of western-central Nepal had worked as a *hali* (bonded tiller) for the Bahuns and Magars of his village for about 20 years. However, when he realised that the work he was doing was humiliating and discriminatory, he stopped working for them, although wage rates had gone up significantly, and he started working independently as a labourer in the construction sector. A woman said that her husband used to work as a *haruwa* (bonded labourer) for a feudal landlord in the village, but she made her husband discontinue this. According to her, 'We had to beg all the time from our owner (*malik*), and only then we got something to eat. Now that he has a different job, he does not need to work under anyone's threat or pressure.' However, she accepted the fact that he became a Haruwa in the past because there was not enough for him to live otherwise. However, his work as Haruwa did not provide sufficient income for the family to survive, which is why she asked him to stop. Her husband now worked in the brick factory in a nearby town and she said that it has been better to run the family this way. This, she thought, had changed the condition of her family: 'Now we also work in sharecropping here and there, and manage our life. In the past, it was always a struggle.' Several families used to work as Haruwa for their landlords, but stopped after the Maoists occupied the land and abolished the system in their village. A Dalit man, 53, worked as Haruwa for a landlord for about 20 years. He gave it up when the local Maoists imposed a ban on the Haruwa system in 2003, and, since then, he has been working as a wage labourer in agriculture and construction for about nine years. A Tharu man, 62, also worked as a Haruwa for a landlord for about 33 years. After being freed of the Haruwa bond, he was now working his land on a sharecropping basis. 'Sharecropping is better, because one would have to work for some certain time and then do other works like wage labour in between.' However, he thinks that the Haruwa system of the past was better, because 'one would get more amount of rice in advance when necessary. But this isn't possible with wage labour type of work. This is why our fathers chose this.' They ended up as Haruwa because the grandfathers and great-grandfathers did not own any land, and there was no alternative, but to work for landlords as Haruwa.

Dalits had to provide labour services to the landowner thrice a year: once during the paddy plantation, once at harvest-time and once for chopping firewood. This system was prevalent among the Sarki community, who were forced to work for the higher caste, as their fathers were debtors to them. However, this has now changed into a system in which labour is exchanged and, sometimes, labour is also hired. Unsurprisingly, landlords feel that these changes have significantly affected their status and, in some cases, they feel that they have been forced to adapt. A Bahun man, whose father was a landlord in the village, felt that Bahun status and prestige had been greatly affected by these changes. According to him, 'In the past, our forefathers (*purkha*) might have dominated them (poor peasants), but at present, these labourers are dominating us.' He further said, 'They have realised that rich people need to rely on them for their existence and, as we cannot do farming on our own, they are further taking advantage of our weakness.' Some of the changes were that, in earlier times, labourers were given one-third of the production and the landowners took two-thirds. However, according to an upper-caste man, 'Labourers are now planning to give one-third to the landowner and keep two-thirds.' Likewise, earlier, labourers working on a sharecropping basis had to deliver paddy to the house of the zamindar (landlord), but now the labourer would do so only if the landlord gave an extra wage. Also, a Bahun man complained, 'No matter how much they (labourers) say, we have to give to them.' Additionally, unlike in the past, even in the sharecropping system, landowners now had to partially cover the cost of fertilisers, and arrange a tractor for ploughing for the labourer. Similarly, a Dalit man opined that labour relations had improved significantly after the restoration of multiparty democracy in 1990. According to him, 'Earlier, labourers had to work all day long, but were not given money on time. They (landlords), indeed, were the true feudal type, who hardly thought of the welfare of their labourers. However, at present, labourers have become much cleverer and are going to retaliate if the landlords try to subjugate the labourers.' In the western Terai, feudal relations have been greatly affected by the Kamaiya movement and peasant liberation. A Tharu man, who once worked as a Kamaiya, but now was free, said, 'My life has changed; although I have many problems at present, I feel good to be free. I work only if I am interested; otherwise, I don't. There isn't any compulsion as there was in the past. Therefore, life is much better than before.' Some Kamaiyas had occupied government land, and some had received support from NGOs to build houses. Those who had not had access to these services were still fighting for their rights and were involved in activism. This had impacted relations with their landlords as most landlords were giving away their land in sharecropping, and some were migrating to urban areas. According to a female bonded labourer, an NGO had been helping them from the beginning to raise awareness and organise the Kamaiya liberation movement. The same NGO had been training them on their right to demand services from the government. However, there were some cases where feudal relations remained strong. A Tharu man had worked as a bonded labourer for the Bahuns of the village for seven years. After the government abolished the system, he continued working for the same Bahuns under a different labour arrangement of sharecropping. He referred to the Bahun as 'mukhiya' or 'malik' ('headman' or 'lord'). Others, like a Dalit couple (aged 49 and 41), had continued the traditional practice of caste-based labour arrangements and preferred them over wage labour as the former offered more security. They had inherited a tailoring job. They had no one in the family who could work on the farms and were not involved in agricultural work; neither did they have land. However, they received grain in return for their work from the landlords in the village. They got about 10 kg of rice each year (collected after the harvest season) from each household who received their services. Some households had increased the quantity of grain and gave 16 kg, while others continued to give 10 kg or even as little as 5 kg. The size of the payment mainly depended on the size of the family of those receiving the service. Understandably, they got more grains from the large families, because they had to sew more clothes than for smaller households. For this couple, the caste-based attached labour system (*balighare*) was better than working as daily wage workers, because one did not have to go and work outdoors. The wife said that they did not have time to sew clothes for wages in addition to providing services to their traditional clients. 'This *balighare* is enough for us,' she said. Although both of them did the tailoring, there seemed to be some division of labour. The husband sewed, while the wife went to the village to collect grains and did other work, such as needlework or fixing buttons. Their adherence to the *balighare* system was guided by the fact that symbolic reciprocity is as important—if not more important—than economic capital. For instance, they could leave the village, get out of the *balighare* system and work in the market doing tailoring. But this was not considered an option, because, as they said, one loses the traditional relationships that one might need in the future. In the time of illness, it is their traditional clients who have helped them, they said. This mutual dependence partly explains why the system has persisted. Giving up traditional practices was not always seen as positive. Working as a *katuwal* (messenger) was all about following in his father's footsteps for a Dalit man we spoke to. He had started working as a messenger in 1999, when his father was getting frail. Others could have replaced his father as the village messenger, but the village elders suggested he should continue his father's job. He thought that the villagers perceived his job positively as he was the medium through which they would know about certain events or activities. He planned to continue working for another 10–12 years. However, with a sarcastic smile, he said, 'I have respect in the village, but of a smaller kind.' He opined that people would not work as *katuwal* for the sake of a little bit of grain, as the amount was unsustainable at the present time. Also, unlike in the past, there were now many opportunities in the village and no compulsion for an individual to work as a *katuwal*. 'If I was enrolled in a government job, then the salary would have increased, but I am still relying on the same quantity of *bali* (grain), which my father used to have.' He got 4–5 kg of rice from each household. He said that the times had changed; for instance, during his father's life, a tiller used to get ₹5, but now they are getting ₹300. He did not perceive his work as exploitative, because he was not forced by the villagers to replace his father. Instead, he decided on his own to do so. Despite the development of modern means of communication, the villagers depended on him for information on certain programmes and events. Therefore, based on social perception, he thought his job had a value in the village. However, he also believed that he was taken for granted by the villagers, as he was treated like a beggar whenever he went to collect the grain every year, and felt humiliated. Due to this minimum value of his work, he will not allow his son to do it, and firmly stated, 'I am not going to let my sons do such work, and would rather send them to India to do labour work.' Besides working as a messenger, he also worked as a wage labourer in a group led by a contractor. The group he belonged to was mostly involved in building small *kacchi* (mud) houses and toilets (the group did not have the skills for making *pakki* houses). Usually, he worked in a group for five months during the winter and throughout the monsoon. Furthermore, during the plantation season, he exchanged labour or worked on a daily wage in agriculture. This case shows that there have been some clear changes in labour relations in rural Nepal that have been directly challenging the traditional, age-old feudal system. Those who had been exercising authority had not only been compelled to give away their power but, in some cases, were forced to meet the labourers' needs and demands. Hence, labourers had also identified the landlords' limitations and had been taking advantage by increasing labour rates. This had subsequently affected the bargaining capacity of the labourers and their relations with their landlords. Although, in some cases, labourers were dependent on their landlords and had established new forms of labour arrangements, the feudal labour system had overall been greatly weakened.

The Commodification of Labour

Previously, rural households were guided by 'reciprocity' when it came to the exchange of labour, a mutual interdependence practice for goods and services. This practice of labour exchange and the reciprocity attached to it did not have any monetary value. Practices of *parima* (labour exchange) were prevalent throughout rural Nepal. The exact value of the labour was not expressed in the labour exchange or attachment system, and it was 'morally wrong' to put a value on the labour. Such exchange and attached forms of labour were beneficial to the landlord or the stronger party, and any exploitation was not questioned. However, since the relationship was built on the exchange of gifts and reciprocity, the landlord or the service user must offer generosity, respect and protection in exchange for the services. Over the years, such reciprocity was normalised as a tradition by both parties leading to the social reproduction of the classes. However, these exchanges have been on the decline as more and more poor peasants are now working on a daily wage basis, either in agriculture and construction, or have migrated. The value of money is also attached to loans, as debtors have started repaying their loans by cash rather than working for others unconditionally. A Magar man worked as a *hali* (bonded tiller) for the Bahuns and Magars in the village because of the loans he had taken. He also worked as a construction worker and as a carpenter. Although he still tilled for others in exchange for grain, he was also involved in non-agricultural work, from which he earned money and had been able to pay back some of the loans to the landlord, and wanted to end that bonded system soon. He said, 'Working as wage labourer is better, because the wage has increased, and I don't have to work for the same person. For better wages, I go to the nearby market, where I can earn as high as ₹500 a day.' In the past, most of the labour work for agriculture was exchanged in kind. Those who worked for the landlords or the others would receive grains and food in kind. This had been replaced by cash for such work. A Dalit woman, 62, who lives with her daughter, has been working in *nimek* (wage labour in agriculture) after her husband died about 17 years ago. That is the main source of income for them. She said, 'When I first started working for others, I would get grains (millets or maize, whatever was available or necessary), but now I get paid in cash. People don't give grains these days.' The wage rate has also increased. As labour becomes scarce due to increased migration out of the villages, there is a demand for labour and, hence, an increase in rates. A high-caste woman complained, saying that the labourers now demand high wages, which are impossible to pay. She said, 'I wanted to hire a tiller, and the person demanded ₹9,000 for one season.'

The availability of food products in nearby markets has influenced the commodification of labour in two ways. First, with the easy availability of food products in nearby markets, there has been a decrease in the farming activities of rural households. The availability of rice in the nearby market has caused people to stop farming in the upper hill region. Second, it means that people need cash to buy products from the market. Cash, available through wage labour or the remittances sent by family members to their households, is the main mode of transaction. People who continued their caste-based occupations were also using cash in exchange for their services. An informant put it like this: '*Balighare chalan* is almost gone, and now everything is exchanged in cash. Earlier, cash was scarce, but now there is a flow of money.' A Dalit couple, who continued to work in the traditional occupation of sewing and provided services for Brahmins and Gurungs, still got grains every year for their tailoring work, although they increasingly preferred cash. Another Dalit man, who worked in the iron workshop (*aran*), was getting grain (*bali*) for his ironwork, but now he preferred to be paid in cash.

Culture of Migration

A focused discussion on the culture of migration in Nepal has been constrained by fragmented scholarship on migration. Existing scholarship categorises migration either by the length of time involved (seasonal, cyclical, permanent, temporary) or in terms of distance (internal, international) or spatial direction (rural-urban, urban-rural, rural-rural) or motivation (voluntary, forced) or in terms of history (historical or modern) and so on. For instance, there exist separate bodies of knowledge on hill-*terai* migration, international labour migration, displacement, trafficking, pilgrimage, child labour or runaway children.

There is a strong tendency to treat different forms of migration as separate and isolated from each other, failing to consider the fluid boundaries between them. Likewise, there is a tendency to contrast the forms of migration—internal versus international, rural to urban versus urban to rural, temporary versus permanent and so on. For instance, there is a lot of literature on migration that is concerned either with internal or international migration, but not both. Internal and international migrations have often been discussed within different theoretical traditions.

When I first embarked on my doctoral field research, such concern with categories was reflected in several interactions with academic and practitioner colleagues, who asked me whether I was researching 'internal' or 'international migration'; 'within Nepal (internal) or outside of Nepal (international)', 'voluntary' or 'forced migration'. Others presumed that I was researching labour migration and asked me, 'Is it to the Gulf or somewhere else? Which country?' and promptly asked questions about the volume and impact of remittances. These concerns demonstrated the popular views of labour mobility from Nepal. Thus, the established categories and typologies of migration have become so authoritative, that, too often, the use of the term 'migration' is limited to include only a certain form of mobility, based on what is considered as having 'significant' temporal, motivational and spatial dimensions. For instance, international, long-distance and permanent mobility is considered more important than internal, short-distance and circular forms of migration.

More critically, the existing categories focus exclusively on the people who move, treating migration primarily as an event in geographical space with very little focus on people's experiences, aspirations and meanings. Moreover, understanding and analysis of mobility have too often been based only on the perspective of those who move without considering how this movement is experienced and understood by the people who stay back, but are also connected to and affected by the mobility. Many wish to out-migrate, but are unable to do so; many plan to migrate and their identities are bound up with this prospect and many find their opportunities constrained or enabled by the migration of their family members, relatives and friends who are preparing to migrate, are migrating or have returned.

Likewise, economic frameworks dominate the discussion on migration, where it is viewed as a dependent variable in the larger equation, involving economic imbalances between different regions and classes, with very little attention paid to the sociocultural dimension of such movement.

There is historical and ethnographic evidence that migration has been a key feature of life and livelihoods in rural Nepal. This includes different forms of labour migration as well as the relocation of households from rural areas to nearby roadside markets or towns or cities. Regardless of caste, ethnicity and class backgrounds, young people are confronted with decision-making on whether, how and when to migrate or stay back. So much so that, outmigration has come to shape, economically and socioculturally, not only those who migrate, but also those who remain (Sharma 2019). Not only does migration offer cash income in the form of remittances, but it also offers a much-needed passage for young people who do not want to remain behind in a situation of joblessness and boredom, and subject to the widespread label of *faltu*[3] (Sharma 2019). Migration is associated with an ability to earn money, often known as *kamaune* in the local idiom (KC 2014), and engage in various forms of consumption. While, historically, migration from Nepal has been associated with landlessness and precarious socio-economic conditions resulting from age-old feudal practices, it is also driven by a desire to take part in consumer activities linked to ideas of modernity. Known as

3 Useless; it was used by unemployed men to talk about their state.

badhyata in literary writings and public culture, the former is seen as a form of compulsion in the context of precarity generated by extractive state policies, landlessness and the caste system. The latter is often referred to as *rahar* in Nepali public culture, a form of desire to experience the world outside and take part in consumer activities associated with earning and spending.

Broadly speaking, there have been three to five waves of migration in or from Nepal (Sharma 2019, Gellner 2013). The first was a direct result of the 18th-century extractive state policies, which forced the peasants to seek livelihoods elsewhere, both within and outside Nepal. This process was not just a result of social transformation within Nepal, but was also informed by the demand for labour in the bordering states of India in sectors such as tea plantation, coal mining, construction, dairy farming, portering in Indian hill stations, domestic employment in middle-class households, agriculture and horticulture (working in orchards). Throughout the fieldwork area, it was possible to find households whose previous generation had migrated to the Indian state of Assam or to Burma, and many relatives had settled there. The second wave of migration started with the recruitment of Nepali men from certain hill ethnic groups by the British Army, which was directly promoted and impacted by colonialism and colonial rule. This practice started after the Treaty of Sagauli in 1816 and was encouraged by the rulers after 1886. This form of migration has been in decline due to factors such as 'less demand for Gorkhas' in the British Army, but also the practice has been challenged by the Nepali Maoists who saw this as an unfair practice in the service of imperialism. Potential recruits from certain hill ethnic groups are increasingly aware of descriptions of the suffering associated with serving in a foreign army, and have, therefore, sought to imagine a future outside foreign army service. This is evident in their increased investment in education as well as participation in the Adivasi Janajati movement, claiming both recognition and the redistribution of economic and political resources from the state. The third wave of migration was again directly linked to precarity of peasant households in Nepal and the demand for labour in Indian cities following decolonisation and processes of modernisation. It became more common for Nepalis, mostly men, to migrate to Indian cities in search of work opportunities in factories, shops and middle-class households. In particular, work was available for Nepali migrants as chowkidar (security guard), which was directly associated with their identity as 'brave Gorkha', domestic help or hotel/restaurant workers (often called *kancha*, which means 'young boy') who were considered to be docile and malleable to the authority of the employers, who are often called owners or *malik* or *sahu* by Nepali migrants, which indicates a feudal form of relationship. The fourth wave of outmigration has been associated with the commodification of labour that started after Nepali citizens gained access to the global labour market. In particular, the introduction of the Labour Act of 1985 and the liberalisation of passport issuance in 1997 promoted this form of outmigration, which has come to shape the nature of the remittance-based national economy of Nepal. Nepali migrant workers are in high demand as temporary workers in the Gulf States or Southeast Asian countries. Likewise, Nepalis from different backgrounds have had high aspirations to migrate to the developed economies of the north, whether as students, refugees or undocumented migrants. The fifth wave of migration, which started after the 1970s, but became much more widespread after the 1990s, followed directly from the first and third waves of migration, where there had been a widespread internal migration to work in informal sectors of the Nepali economy, such as brick kilns, construction, small-scale factories, domestic work, transport, service sector work in hospitality sectors such as hotels and restaurants in markets, towns and cities.

Precarities

While the overall political-economic transition from feudal to non-feudal working relationships has been beneficial, there are disparities in how these benefits have been distributed. For young people, in particular, the new dispensation offers opportunities that did not previously exist to escape from the regimented order of traditional village life. For them, the diversification resulting from the weakening of the feudal system and its attendant structural violence has been a plus. Migration, non-agricultural wage labour and employment in the informal services sector represent both aspirations and opportunities for change. However, migration does not automatically offer an exit from unfreedom to freedom. The circular migrants are often caught in an exploitative cycle of deception, debt, ill-treatment and humiliation with no guaranteed economic return for many. Likewise, some groups are left behind by the gradual weakening of the reciprocal relationships inherent in the feudal caste system, which were exploitative at the core, but provided a form of safety net in times of need. Those who are too old, weak or ill to adapt, or lack marketable skills face perhaps greater vulnerabilities than before. The people who stay behind look after the household and care for the old, the sick and children; however, in the absence of a social safety net, many are exposed to new forms of precarity. Two Dalit sisters in a hill village spoke about how they could barely survive on the daily wage they earn, working on others' farms. They have a tiny piece of land, and a portion of it has been taken away by a recent landslide. The sisters have no skills beyond agriculture, and it is difficult for them to manage; moreover, the traditional form of insurance, based on client-patron relations, has eroded. It is the women, the elderly and destitute groups, who are more vulnerable due to the ongoing transitions in labour.

The coronavirus pandemic of 2019 made the vulnerability of Nepali migrants visible like never before. Images and reports of tens and thousands of distressed Nepali migrant workers, in India, attempting to make long journeys home by foot and stranded in transport hubs and border points, were widely circulated in the media along with stories of lost jobs, humiliation and ill treatment. In the context of the pandemic and uncertainties in the destination, it was only natural for these migrants to attempt to return home. Eventually, the migrants were allowed to travel, cross the border and return to their families. Distressed and stranded, Nepali migrant workers returning from India, when interviewed by journalists, spoke about the humiliation, difficulties and uncertainties, and many vowed never to return to work in India. Politicians, intellectuals and policymakers in the capital spoke enthusiastically with nationalistic sentiments about how this return would open opportunities for reviving rural agriculture and employment opportunities in Nepal. Rhetoric aside, within three months, many people had begun to return to India in search of work, despite the rapid rise in coronavirus cases in the country. Such is the reality in rural Nepal, where, despite perceived risks, poorer households are left with little choice but to migrate.

While labour mobility has provided opportunities for many, migrants who travel away are often faced with insecurity, discrimination and poor working/living conditions. Healthcare expenses and fraud and extortion while travelling are major concerns among migrant workers. They are often paid less than promised, and barely manage to make savings to send home, not to mention constant peer pressure to spend money on alcohol and expensive mobile phones. Labourers are often subject to extortion, especially when their work involves several middlemen. A Tharu man from Terai, who worked as a construction worker in a hill village, felt that working in a new place made him vulnerable, as he did not receive his money on time. As the family relied on the cash income from the breadwinner, illness was a significant worry. Sickness and the associated cost of medicine consistently emerged as a major cause of concern among the labouring population. In the absence of any social protection, many could not bear the cost of medicines required during illness and took out loans. A man who used to work as a daily wage worker in a Terai district was injured at work and had been prescribed medicine for four years. In addition to taking loans to pay for his medical bills, he had to rely on his wife's wage labour to help the family survive. Likewise, households who had lost their male breadwinner were facing serious difficulties. A Dalit woman from a hill village in far-western Nepal had lived with her husband in an Indian city; however, eight years ago she lost him in a tragic accident, which forced her to return to Nepal. She did not have any land back in the village and, thus, relied on wage labour to support her three children. Her only expectation was to see her son become old enough to travel to India and earn money for the family. A woman from a hill village was working as a wage labourer in a town in western-central Nepal, leaving behind her two children in the village. Her husband worked in Mumbai in India, but since he never sent money or returned home, she has to maintain her family by herself, leaving her children in the care of their grandparents. Poor pay and underpayment for migrant workers directly contribute to precarities back in the village, as the family left behind have to look after the household plus any old, sick or very young dependents.

The following two ethnographic vignettes explore migrant precarities in more details.

In 2012, I visited a brick kiln, located just off the main highway going out of Kathmandu, some 30 minutes from the city. One of the first sights was the smoke coming out of a chimney, small huts made with bricks, stacks of bricks, raw and cooked, and many people moving around, doing different things. Brick kilns, some 700 of them located throughout Nepal, each employing 300–500 workers, employ internal migrants from different parts of Nepal. Employment in this sector is directly related to the construction boom in Nepal. Located on the outskirts of the city or market areas, the brick kiln is a place that has a 'camp-like', temporary feel. It is a place where workers live and work day and night, and are continuously under their supervisors' surveillance. There is very little separation between private and public life in these kilns. It is possible to see the workers carrying bricks, moulding, baking and even cooking, washing, sleeping and playing at any one time. Two boys, aged 10–12, were mixing the mud and making dough; another young girl, aged around 12, was drying the bricks and counting them. Three young children, about 2–3 years old, were playing around in the same area. Workers in the brick kilns, almost all of whom are seasonal migrants from rural areas, constitute not only one of the poorest and weakest sections of the labouring population, they are also susceptible to low pay, difficult and unhealthy working conditions and exploitation. The wage rates do not reflect the degree of exploitation, bearing in mind that the child and women workers often remain as the invisible workforce both in the worksite or back home. The workers come to work in the kilns through a middleman or contractor called a *naike*. The recruitment of the labour force through the *naike* is arranged through a system of advance payment called *peshki*. The *naike*'s role is to arrange and supply a labour force to the kiln, arrange advance payment, supervise them and settle the workers' financial accounts. An individual or an entire family (excluding old, disabled and dependent persons), comprising husband, wife and children, may be recruited to the brick kilns and work as one unit for the full season of the operating kiln.

The employees' work record is updated every week (during the weekly day-off), and they are provided with a certain amount weekly, called *haphta*, for their subsistence. These amounts do not match the value of their work and their due wages for what they have produced. They receive only about a quarter of their wages on a regular basis. The money given to them towards expenses and the advance they have taken are deducted at the end of the season, when the final payment is made. In a way, the owners and the contractors retain the workers until they have earned enough to pay back the advance and the amount given as expenses. It is not easy for workers to leave the kiln, when they wish to look for alternative work opportunities. The labourers work on contract and piece basis. Hence, the people, who are strong enough, carry more or work more, and can make more money than the others. Therefore, it is very easy for the workers to self-exploit. The moulders, loaders and unloaders normally work for 12–14 hours daily with between half and a full day off per week.

The day starts early for the kiln workers, perhaps as early as 5 AM. They take a break for lunch for 1–2 hours and then work again until late evening. Although it was a day off in the kiln, on this visit, a man was mixing mud to make a dough. When asked why he was working on a day off, he replied that he does not take days off. The man was 44 years old, but looked about 60. He was skinny, looked malnourished and extremely fatigued. He had a 15-month-old baby and wife with him. The three of them lived in a small hut, made up of raw bricks, next to where he was working. As he was making dough, he was sweating. The work he was doing was not necessarily skilled. Both he and his wife made bricks, and his wife worked to dry them and stack them. Apart from making bricks, he also carried bricks in the kiln to earn extra money. Before coming to work in the brick kiln in Kathmandu, he used to work in Pokhara, carrying and loading sand for construction. Although he could earn more money in his previous work, he came to work in the kiln because the family can live and work together as a production unit. Both he and his wife got work, and the work was on a piece basis, so there was no wage difference for men and women. In our conversation, he told me that the couple might make 1,500–2,000 bricks per day, that is, around 10,000 bricks per week, which earned them about रू7,000 per week, but only if they worked every single day from morning to evening. Working hours are lost during winter rains, not to mention other work stoppages arbitrarily decided by kiln owners or dictated by a reduction in demand for bricks. There are no workplace standards, when it comes to working in brick kilns. The work does not offer a bonus or provident funds, maternity leave, protective gear, gratuities or medical benefits. Workers are not compensated for days when work stops because of rain or for some other reason.

From a brick kiln in Kathmandu, let's turn our attention to Delhi, where a group of young migrant workers from mid-western Nepal work in a cramped momo restaurant in the vicinity of an upper-class neighbourhood. It was just before 9 AM in the summer of 2012, and the restaurant had not opened for business. The takeaway restaurant was located on the ground floor of the building and served momos, noodles and similar items. There were a couple of rented rooms on the second floor of the building where the workers, all from mid-western Nepal, lived and worked. The owner, who was also a Nepali from the same region of Nepal, had been bringing workers from the same area since he began his business about 12 years ago. As we climbed the stairs and made it to the second floor, there were three young boys chopping onions and cabbage in large quantities to prepare momos in a very dark, wet and humid room, and one of them was washing the cooking utensils from the previous day. It was extremely hot, with no ventilation, and the boys were sweating. On the left side was a room with several beds on the floor, covered by unarranged bed sheets. These boys worked and lived there, and mostly there was no life for them beyond working in this kitchen, except for the occasional trip to the nearby shop to purchase onions, vegetables and other grocery items, or to watch films once in a while. These boys worked long hours, starting as early as 7 AM and continuing to work till 11 PM or 12 AM, and there was no weekend or time-off for them. They woke up in the morning, cleaned the kitchen, washed all the utensils, brought large quantities of vegetables and other supplies from a wholesale shop, did all the preparatory work, including chopping and making momos, and one or two of them delivered the cooked meals to different stalls and homes in the neighbourhood. Those who went for home delivery bathed, and wore a clean t-shirt and a cap. These boys earned about ₹2,500–3,000 per month.

Overall, although the idea of freedom appears to be driving much of the outmigration from rural Nepal, as seen in the above cases, mobility and wage labour often lead to contradictory class mobility, that is, while migration has undoubtedly opened up opportunities for cash income, the nature of the work and the working conditions often result in suffering. In many ways, one could argue that the social suffering that migrants experience in the destination is just an extension of what they aspire to escape from in Nepal's rural villages. The paradox is that migrants escape from semi-feudal or bonded conditions in the village and then find themselves in equally exploitative, if not semi-feudal, working conditions in the migratory process and at the destination.

Conclusion

First, rural Nepal is on the cusp of a major transformation from a relatively stable condition of reproduction of social and economic relations based on agriculture, land, feudal and caste structures to a more fluid and open condition, where the old 'order' is rapidly changing, if not collapsing. People's livelihoods and rural social relations, even in the most remote locations, are increasingly affected by the circulation of labour, migrant remittances, the incorporation of the rural economy into globalised flows and the commodification of labour and land, to name but a few factors. The labour exodus from agriculture and the countryside has now become a regular phenomenon. The opening up of the countryside to the outside world, the improved road network and exposure to other forms of modernity have accelerated labour mobility on a larger scale than ever before. The labour shortage in rural Nepal has bestowed increased bargaining power on the labouring population. Consequently, migration and remittance have directly and indirectly weakened the land-based and caste-based attached labour and social relations.

Second, circulation and multilocality are key features of a mobile livelihood's strategy for an increasingly large number of households. Migrants remain embedded in their village of origin through repeated visits and keeping up with village social networks. They are accepted in the urban centres only as temporary workers and keep up ties with the village as insurance if they fail to find other work. Likewise, migrants depend extensively on social and caring support provided by their families back in the village. One of the paradoxes of such a circulatory form of migration is that the identity of the migrant remains attached to the village, even if the working sites and sectors are modern and urban. Overall, while the idea of freedom away from the regimented and constrained life in the village has been driving much of outmigration from rural Nepal, the mobility of labour has not necessarily meant more freedom for poorer migrants (Sharma 2019). The attached forms of labour, embedded in social relationships, caste and patronage, are now being replaced with flexible and self-exploitative forms, without minimal social and economic protection. Escaping the old ties of bondage and attachment has certainly led to optimism and some positive outcomes in terms of the freedom to move. However, migration can also be an integral part of unfree labour. There are remarkable similarities in the ways unfreedom manifests, whether in sectors of the economy, such as brick kilns or domestic work within Nepal or overseas labour migration.

Thirdly, as they attempt to escape a difficult economic situation back in the village, migrant workers land in a work setting and living conditions in cities and other destinations that are highly exploitative. The poorer sections of the population from rural Nepal end up migrating to nearby towns or cities to work in brick kilns, construction, domestic situations, hotels/restaurants, factories (for example, carpet and garment) and small-scale manufacturing that exists in and around towns in the Terai, or across the border in India. Others, especially those who can mobilise economic, political and social capital, seek to migrate to international destinations, such as the Gulf States or South-East Asian countries. For most, their work is characterised by low pay, piece-rate payment, unskilled or underskilled work, intermittent work and no written contract or social protection. Their living and working conditions, perpetuated by their racialised and classed identity, exposes them to ill health and ill treatment. Yet, there are no promising regulatory or social protection mechanisms to protect migrant workers in these circumstances.

References

Adhikari, J. 2001. 'Mobility and Agrarian Change in Central Nepal'. *Contributions to Nepalese Studies*, 28: 247–267.

Adhikari, J. and M. Hobley. 2015. '"Everyone is Leaving: Who Will Sow Our Fields?" The Livelihood Effects on Women of Male Migration from Khotang and Udaypur Districts, Nepal, to the Gulf Countries and Malaysia'. *Himalaya, the Journal of the Association for Nepal and Himalayan Studies*, 35(1): 11–23.

Blaikie, P., J. Cameron, and D. Seddon. 1980. *Nepal in Crisis: Growth and Stagnation at the Periphery*. Delhi: Oxford University Press.

Blaikie, P., J. Cameron, and D. Seddon. 2002. 'Understanding 20 Years of Change in West-Central Nepal: Continuity and Change in Lives and Ideas'. *World Development* 30: 1255–1270.

Campbell, B. 2018. 'Moral Ecologies of Subsistence and Labour in a Migration Affected Community of Nepal'. *Journal of the Royal Anthropological Institute*, 24 (S1):151–165.

Caplan, L. 1990. *Land and Social Change in East Nepal: A Study of Hindu-Tribal Relations*. London: Routledge and Kegan Paul.

Caplan, P. 1972. *Priests and Cobblers: A Study of Social Change in a Hindu Village in West Nepal*. London: Intertext.

Chhetri, R.B. 2005. 'The Plight of the Tharu Kamaiyas in Nepal: A Review of the Social, Economic and Political Facets'. *Occasional Papers in Sociology and Anthropology*, 9: 22–46.

Gellner, D.N. 2013. 'Warriors, Workers, Traders, and Peasants: The Nepali/Gorkhali Diaspora since the Nineteenth Century'. In *Routledge Handbook of South Asian Diasporas*, edited by D. Washbrook and J. Chatterjee, 136–150. Abingdon and New York: Routledge.

Giri, B.R. 2010. 'Bonded Labour Practice in Nepal: The Promise of Education As a Magnet of Child Bondedness'. *South Asia Research*, 30(2):145–164.

Hitchcock, J.T. 1961. 'A Nepalese Hill Village and Indian Employment'. *Asian Survey*, 1(9): 15–20.

Holmberg, D. and K. March. 1999. 'Local Production/ Local knowledge: Forced Labour from Below'. *Studies in Nepali History and Society*, 4(1): 5–64.

KC, G. 2014. *Kamaune: The Cultural and Economic Imaginaries of Migration*. CESLAM: Kathmandu.

Macfarlane, A. 1976. *Resources and Population: A Study of Gurungs of Nepal*. London: Cambridge University Press.

Macfarlane, A. 2001. 'Sliding Downhill: Some Reflections on Thirty Years of Change in a Himalayan Village'. *European Bulletin for Himalayan Research*, 20: 105–110.

Mishra, C. 2010. *Badalindo Nepali Samaj*. Kathmandu: Fine Prints.

Onta, P. 1994. '*Rich Possibilities: Notes on Social History* in Nepal'. *Contributions to Nepalese Studies*, 21: 1–43.

Panter-Brick, C., M. Eggerman. 1997. 'Household Responses to Food Shortages in Western Nepal'. *Human Organization*, 56(2): 190–198.

Pfaff-Czarnecka, Joanna. 1995. 'Migration Under Marginality Conditions: The Case of Bajhang'. *Rural-Urban Interlinkages: A Challenge for Swiss Development Cooperation*, edited by I.A. IDA, 97–108. Zurich, INFRAS.

Raj, Y. 2010. *History As Mindscapes: A Memory of the Peasants' Movement of Nepal*. Kathmandu: Martin Chautari.

Regmi, M.C. 1961. 'Recent Land Reforms in Nepal'. *Asian Survey*, 1(7): 32–37.

Regmi, M.C. 1976. *Landownership in Nepal*. University of California Press.

Regmi, M.C. 1978. *Thatched Huts and Stucco Palaces: Peasants and Landlords in the 19th Century Nepal*. New Delhi: Vikas.

Regmi, M.C. 1988. *An Economic History of Nepal, 1846–1901*. Varanasi: Nath.

Seddon, D., J. Adhikari, and G. Gurung. 2001. *The New Lahures: Foreign Employment and Remittance Economy of Nepal*. Kathmandu: NIDS.

Sharma, J.R. 2008. 'Practices of Male Labour Migration from the Hills of Nepal to India in Development Discourses: Which Pathology?'. *Gender, Development and Technology*, 12(3): 303–323.

Sharma, J.R. 2019. *Crossing the Border to India: Youth, Migration and Masculinities in Nepal*. New Delhi: Bloomsbury.

Shrestha, N.R. 2001. *The Political Economy of Land, Landlessness and Migration in Nepal*. New Delhi: Nirala.

Shrestha, N.R. 2008. '"Misery is My Company Now": Nepal's Peasantry in the Face of Failed Development'. *The Journal of Peasant Studies*, 35(3): 452–475.

Sunam, R. 2014. 'Marginalised *Dalits* in International Labour Migration: Reconfiguring Economic and Social Relations in Nepal'. *Journal of Ethnic and Migration Studies*, 40(12): 2030–2048.

A protest in Kathmandu, 2007

4

Mobility and Educational and Occupational Futures

Over the last three decades, the desire of Nepali youth from all genders, castes, classes and ethnicities to migrate to towns and cities in search of higher education and secure employment has never been higher. The idea of *bikas* in Nepal has had the effect of creating a view of Nepali villages as traditional settlements to be left in the past and urban areas as modern places to be desired, and this is shaping the aspirations and patterns of mobility of the Nepali youth (Pigg 1992, Sharma 2019). Remittance flow to rural households, from overseas labour migration, has supported investment in education and the movement of youth to cities. Promotion of schooling, as a part of global campaigns such as 'Education for All', and adoption of inclusive policies in education and affirmative action adopted by the Government of Nepal has significantly contributed to the transformation of the demographic composition in schooling. These various factors have resulted in higher school enrolment rates for traditionally marginalised groups such as Dalits, ethnic groups and women (Stash and Hannum 2001). Historically, giving importance to education has been a feature of upper-caste men reaffirming their dominance in higher-level educational attainment and social and political networks, leading them to secured salaried government jobs and political positions. However, in the recent decades, there has been an increase in the aspirations and patterns of mobility of women and men from historically disadvantaged castes, classes and ethnicities in search of education and secure salaried jobs to the cities.

Yet, secure salaried jobs are scarce, leading to tough competition. Furthermore, young men from different castes, classes and ethnicities are differently equipped to navigate pathways to higher education and secure employment in the cities. Sluggish job creation has resulted in a large number of unemployed young men, and many may have little choice other than seeking to out-migrate in search of jobs as migrant workers.

In this context, this chapter focuses on the experience of young men from rural Nepal, with diverse caste, class and ethnicity, as they seek to navigate and realise their educational and occupational aspirations, and as they struggle to overcome challenges in the process of mobility to the city. More broadly, it examines youth mobility to cities for education and employment, against the backdrop of limited jobs, the radical restructuring of the Nepali state and broader development processes. The questions this chapter aims to answer are: What are the patterns of youth mobility from different castes, classes and ethnicities to the city? How do young men and women from rural areas navigate and realise their educational and occupational futures? How does mobility to the city produce and reproduce subjectivities among youth? Answering these questions may help us understand how youth mobility to cities may be contributing to the restructuring of the state from below.

The material for this chapter is primarily drawn from my fieldwork in a village in Palpa district and following young men, who travelled to the town of Tansen and the city of Kathmandu, two key destinations for attaining higher education and seeking employment. Over the years, there has been a marked transformation in higher education aspirations among the youth from rural areas. I start by discussing the changing meanings of higher education and salaried employment for young men from upper-caste Bahun, Dalits and Magars from the village. Then, I will discuss how Bahun, Dalit and Magar men from the village navigate their journey to the city and the likely impact this journey has on their subjectivities. Through this, I discuss how historical disadvantage and privilege, associated with caste, class, gender and ethnicity on the one hand, and opportunities as well as challenges for achievement and success on the other, are produced and reproduced through mobility for education and employment to urban centres. Finally, I will discuss the impact of this mobility on the caste and ethnic subjectivities among the rural youth.

Social Meanings and Patterns of Mobility

Outmigration in search of education and employment among the youth is a regular feature in Nepali villages. Moreover, it is not just limited to the 'overseas labour migration' that has come to lately dominate the academic, public and policy debates in Nepal (Seddon et al. 2001). As the ideas of *bikas* have penetrated the rural areas, primarily through schooling and other aspects of modernity, young men and women have sought to navigate journeys to the towns and cities inside Nepal in search of educational and occupational futures.

The phrase *padhna jane* was used to talk about those who went out of the village to acquire educational qualifications. This mobility was significant, as it resulted in securing jobs, providing opportunities for socio-economic mobility for the household and, occasionally, led to the relocation of the entire household.

Education was valued more by the Bahuns than the Magars and Dalits, and more among males than females. From the perspective of Bahun men, education was an important aspect of their priestly identity and secured salaried jobs. The Bahun children were brought up with expectations that they would acquire educational qualifications, which would play an important role in their futures. In recent years, a few Magars have begun to send their children for education to Tansen and Kathmandu, primarily because they think education leads to more opportunities and is considered an important route to development. This was reflected in the sentiments of some Magars, who felt that they were left behind due to the lack of education. There was an emerging discourse among Magars in Palpa, popularised by Maoist activists, that they lagged behind in development, as they did not invest in education and prized recruitment in a foreign army. Historically, Dalits from Palpa lagged behind in schooling and education. Dalits had begun to view education as a source of freedom from the everyday life of caste in the village and to send their children to the village school. However, the dropout rate remained very high, as economic needs meant that Dalit young men began to work either locally or migrated early.

The process of education had changed over the years, allowing new patterns and new actors. Parents seek to finance their children's education with the expectation that these children will later find employment and contribute to the household's security. Increasingly, investment in education in the cities became a strategy that was adopted not only by Bahun, but also Magar, households, who used their remittances or sold a part of their property to pay for their children's education. The investment includes fees and costs associated with travel and living. Dalit households have begun to view education as a route to social mobility, but, except for a couple of households, most do not have the social and political networks needed to migrate to the city for education. Gaining a good education (outside Palpa) is expensive, and it was only the wealthy or those of high status, who already had networks in Kathmandu or elsewhere, who were able to do it. The children, in return, were expected to study hard and obtain a job that would guarantee the security of the family. Education in the cities was usually supported by close relatives, who often provided guidance and, in some cases, offered accommodation.

Mobility for further education in colleges and universities was significant. In addition to leading to educational qualifications, mobility to the city offered them a new network of friends and exposed them to new life experiences. Those who went to college and universities discovered a new political environment. Some of them took part in political organisations and became politically active. This exposure introduced them to new ideologies and aspirations, which again changed their relationship with home.

Many young people who left for further education lived permanently outside of the village. Unlike in the past, young men did not necessarily come back to the village after completing their studies. Instead, they remained in the cities, mainly in Tansen and Kathmandu, searching for employment opportunities. The departure from the village to urban centres for education, in most cases, meant permanent mobility, leading to relocation to the city. Earlier, salaried jobs were mainly available in government departments. However, in recent years, salaried jobs had become available in towns and cities in private firms, NGOs and other service sectors, although these jobs were not always secure. Fierce competition for salaried employment meant that only a few individuals could succeed, and the rest had to look for other jobs within or outside Nepal.

Mobility to the city for education was directly associated with the search for salaried employment. People used the terms *jagire khana jane* (meaning 'to eat *jagire*', that is, land) or *nokari garna jane* (meaning 'to work as servants') to talk about the mobility of men and women, who went to work in professional or semi-professional jobs. The terms *jagire* and *nokari* covered the jobs that were more or less permanent or, in some cases, temporary, but ensured a degree of job security and ensured regular payment. Mostly, the term *jagire* was used to talk about civilian jobs within Nepal. However, it was also used with reference to anyone working within or outside of Nepal. For example, those who worked outside of Nepal in salaried jobs, including those recruited in the army, were also known as *jagires*.

The term *jagire* was a form of land assignment in return for state service, a common means of payment to soldiers in the Nepali Army in the 19th century. Although these days people, employed by the state or private agencies, did not get paid in the form of land, most of them used the salary to purchase land, which signified their particular relationship to the state as servants. At the same time, a few people from outside the village were employed in the village in the school, health post and village administration.

To have someone employed was a matter of great pride and prestige for the entire household, and determined the household's location in the village's socio-economic and moral hierarchy. The income from a regular salary played a significant role in the upward socio-economic mobility of these *jagire* individuals and their households. Most importantly, it was the security of consistent income that was highly valued by the households. From the perspective of the *jagire* individuals, it was a matter of great pride to have found employment and earned respect among friends and relatives.

Having someone employed opened up new possibilities for the household, including facilitating the education of the other members or helping other family members find employment in the cities through newly established networks. The older household members considered that it was the *jagire* member's responsibility to 'do something' (*kehi gardine*), usually, for the younger members like brother/nephew (*bhai/bhatija*) in the household or other close relatives.

Jagire khane was so crucial to village life that the parents of girls would particularly look for a *jagire* to marry their daughter. The first inquiry made by the parents of the girl would be 'whether the man was employed or not'. Only when the parents knew that the person had employment would they inquire about the type of employment. A good job meant that the boy's household could arrange a marriage with the girl of their choice.

In rural Palpa, except for a few wealthy upper-caste households that sent their children to residential boarding schools or other private schools in nearby towns, like Tansen and Butwal, or Kathmandu, most young men completed primary and secondary schooling in the village, before moving to the city. For richer households, schooling in the cities from the foundational years had important symbolic and instrumental value as it was a practice through which they sought to distinguish their status from others and, more importantly, it was a route to secure their children's occupational futures in the context of growing competition for salaried jobs. Unlike the past, when rural landholding was associated with power, from the vantage point of wealthy rural households, in the changing economic and political context, power was increasingly related to educational qualifications from respected institutions, owning land and property in cities and eventual relocation to the city. In Palpa, the affluent households had invested in a plot of land or building houses in the towns and cities, even though they continued to live in the rural area. Investment in their children's education in English-medium schools in cities was a key route to secure employment opportunities in emerging sectors of the economy, such as banks, financial institutions, NGOs and service sectors.

One of the wealthiest households in the fieldwork area had arranged for two sons and one daughter to complete their education in Kathmandu. Initially, they sent their eldest son from the age of five to boarding schooling in Butwal while the younger son and daughter started their schooling in the village. Later, the family rented a flat and admitted their younger son in a reputed school in Tansen, while the daughter continued to go to the primary school in the village, reflecting the gendered calculations of the household. Eventually, when the eldest son finished his high school with a distinction from the boarding school, the family decided to rent a flat close to one of their relatives in Kathmandu and sent all three children for education to Kathmandu. The eldest son went on to study medicine, the youngest son studied engineering and the daughter went to a private school, all of which required a significant amount of money, which the family could afford. Eventually, the family built a house in Kathmandu and relocated there. Having completed their educational qualifications, the two sons secured high-paying secure jobs in Kathmandu and their daughter was married to a Nepali man, who settled in the US. This family had extensive property in the village in Palpa and in the Terai, which their grandfather had secured as *birta*, and had built social and political networks that extended to cities beyond the village, which made it possible for the parents' investment in their children's education and their futures.

Similarly, another rich Magar family, in which the father had served in the British Army, had relocated to Kathmandu as they sought to invest in their children's education in private schools in the city. The father, who had retired from the army but continued to work in security companies overseas, eventually relocating to the UK, spoke about the importance of good quality education for their children. He justified his 'hard work' overseas for their children's future and did not want to send his son for recruitment in a foreign army. He wanted his daughter not to be married to a *lahure*,[1] but to an educated man, who had a secure job. Having bought a property in Kathmandu, the daughter and the son went to one of the best schools in the city. The daughter completed an MPhil degree in Social Sciences and eventually worked for international NGOs in Kathmandu. The son studied business management and began his own business.

The poorer households had very little choice, other than to send their children to the village school. A few sent their children for further education to a government college in Tansen, which did not guarantee secure employment. Some of those who went to study in government colleges found themselves applying for teaching jobs or low-ranking government jobs, while others eventually migrated overseas. Kamal, a Bahun man, came to study in Tansen for his higher education. Having completed his undergraduate degree in economics after failing a couple of times, he applied for low-ranking civil service

1 This term is associated with Nepali men recruited into a foreign army. The term *lahure* came from the name of the city of Lahore in Pakistan. It was originally used to refer to the hill men who went to Lahore to work in the Sikh leader Ranjit Singh's army in the early 19th century. The term *lahure* has become the everyday term to refer to anyone going to work abroad, whether for army work or not, but the typical *lahure* is still perceived to be the army man. For a deeper ethnography on *lahure*, see: Adhikari (1993) and Des Chene (1991).

jobs, but could not secure one. He returned to the village to work as a temporary teacher for a couple of years with the help of his father, a teacher in the village. Later, he went to Qatar to find work, but returned, as he became very ill and lost weight significantly.

A couple of families had sent their children to work as domestic workers in affluent households in cities, like Tansen and Kathmandu, in exchange for education, social and political networks, and a better future. One of them, a Bahun boy, had managed to complete his schooling with first division, and, with the 'source and force' of the employer family, he had secured a job in a government bank. Another Magar boy did not manage to finish his school as expected and had ended up working as a delivery driver in Kathmandu.

An overall trend that was on the decline was that children from poorer households dropped out of school and began to take full-time adult responsibilities by working on farms, while a few young boys dropped out of school and ran away to India (*bhagne*). It was common for Dalit households in the village to have their children drop out of school and work as daily wage labourers in agriculture or migrate to find work in India. Similarly, poorer Bahun and Magar households who could not afford to send their older children for high school or further education sent them to work as migrant workers in India or to work as wage labourers in the village.

Young men's struggle to secure educational and occupation futures was not of their own making. There was a direct relationship between caste, class, ethnicity and access to education and salaried jobs. For instance, investment in higher education, civil service, teaching and other forms of salaried employment in the private sector and NGOs within Nepal had been common among the Bahuns. When Magars had begun to invest in children's education, service in a foreign army or police or overseas migration had been common among this community, with a few of them working as teachers and NGO workers in the village. Dalits mainly worked as labourers in agriculture or migrated to India; however, a few had begun to complete high school in the village, and one had found a temporary job locally with an NGO. Nonetheless, the aspiration for education was very high among the Dalit households, who saw that schooling was important for improving their life chances.

In 2005, my household survey of 160 households (70 Bahun, 70 Magar and 20 Dalit) showed that 18 individuals (15 men and 3 women), comprising 15 Bahuns and 3 Magars, had moved out of the village for salaried employment in different parts of Nepal. No Dalits had moved out for salaried jobs. Among the Magars, out of 70 Magar households, 14 households had *lahure*s working with the Indian Army and three households had *lahure*s working with the British Army. While I did not conduct a similar survey in 2015, aspirations for education and employment were clearly very high among the Magars and Dalits in the village.

Earlier, a few Bahun men from the village had gone to Tansen, Banaras and Kathmandu for their schooling and returned home upon completing their education to work locally as priests, teachers and government employees. For them, it was important to move away for education, so that they could return to the village and hold some important positions locally. Upon securing salaried jobs, Bahun men from Palpa also went to work for the government in the nearby towns or other parts of Nepal, mainly as teachers and civil servants. In Palpa, except for a very few poor households, all men from Bahun households had at least one person pursuing further education or a job outside the village. A few Bahun men had gone to work overseas, and a few had also gone to work as manual labourers in India. While the Magars historically sought to work in a foreign army, more were now migrating for further education and sought jobs in the government, NGOs and the private sector. Dalit men from the village had begun to go to the towns and cities in search of education and jobs. In the fieldwork area, two Dalit boys had gone to Tansen and Kathmandu for education and employment, and most Dalit households sent their children to the local secondary school.

Navigating the City

For young men from rural areas, the city was a completely different space. Not only did they carry their rural identity, but they were also poorly equipped to navigate and experience their life in the city.

Embarking on an educational journey and finding employment in the context of limited jobs was extremely difficult as it involved hard work, apart from securing academic qualifications from a reputed institution. After completing their education in cities like Tansen and Kathmandu, most young men extended their stay until they managed to find work. Commonly known as *jagir khojne*, finding jobs was extremely difficult and did not always result in secure salaried employment.

For many, it resulted in repeated frustration and landing in precarious jobs. In other cases, where the young men could not find employment within Nepal, they left to work in the Gulf States or the South East Asian countries.

I met several students pursuing higher education in Kathmandu and Tansen, who wanted to see their education leading to salaried jobs and none of them were interested in going back to the village, without securing salaried employment. The value of higher education was viewed in terms of its potential to provide salaried employment opportunities. As their families in the village had funded their education, these young men found it very difficult to ask for money from home as soon as their study came to an end, and there was a sense of urgency to find employment, so that they could manage to stay in the city without being dependent on the family. Due to stiff competition for jobs, it was common to see many men and women desperately looking for jobs after completion of their studies. Many of them did not want to be seen as *faltu*, but preferred to work in any form of employment they could find. Many of them worked in underpaid jobs, mostly as teachers and tutors in private boarding schools and tuition centres, or under precarious contracts in Kathmandu's emergent service sectors, on salaries that were barely enough to manage their day-to-day expenses. They continued to work with the hope that they would be able to find a better job someday. Many of them had no choice, but to continue asking for money from their parents or elder siblings, until they found a job. In the meantime, a few of them found it difficult to be seen as unemployed, but instead preferred to enrol on another degree course or gain other qualifications, such as one in English language or computing.

Those seeking posts had to respond to jobs advertised in the newspapers by sending out a series of applications and looking for *source force*.[2] It was common to see them browsing through newspapers to look for a suitable vacancy. One man aged 31 told me that he had spent thousands of rupees taking application print-outs, preparing his CV and sending out application letters by post. After applying for posts, most jobseekers were never called for an interview, which they thought was because of the lack of a recommendation. A job was always possible with a recommendation from an influential person (usually a politician, senior bureaucrat or other influential personality). These applicants had to assess whether a recommendation from a particular person would be strong enough or not. Before applying for jobs, these men would often check in their family/kinship or political networks to try to find the right channel to get their message across. Men I spoke to believed that it was necessary to pay a bribe to find a job.

While some jobseekers developed connections using their kinship network in the city, others developed connections using a friendship or a political affiliation developed in the university. Those who got permanent salaried employment worked till they retired, mostly at the age of 58 or 60. For those in temporary jobs, the period varied;

2 It referred to a kin network for a recommendation, which was needed for finding a job. It was also called *bhansun*.

they worked for a few years in one place and found another job thereafter. The *jagire* spent most of their time away from home. Depending on the nature of the employment, some of them were posted to one place for life, while others moved to different locations as required by the jobs. Only a few found positions close to their home and some of them who found a salaried job in Tansen preferred to commute daily.

Mahesh, a young Bahun man, completed his schooling in the village and commuted to Tansen for college. Once his elder brother found a job in Kathmandu at a travel agency, he transferred his college to Kathmandu and lived with his elder brother. While his elder brother worked and studied, Mahesh completed his education from a government college while cooking and cleaning for himself and his brother. Having finished his degree, he applied for several jobs only to be rejected. He and his brother made numerous visits to their relatives and people in their social and political networks from the village in Kathmandu for tea, to attempt to secure Mahesh a job. Having completed his education from the village school and government college, Mahesh was not well prepared for the highly competitive job market in Kathmandu. Although he studied law, he soon realised that he did not have the confidence or the networks needed to practise law. He spent years trying for the civil service, while simultaneously trying for jobs everywhere else. Both the brothers subscribed to *Kantipur*, a popular newspaper, to search for job vacancies and sent extensive applications only to be rejected. His brother found him a clerical job in a migrant recruitment agency in Kathmandu that did not pay much, but at least he had a job and got married. Once married, he was under pressure to earn money to pay for their expenses. He decided to go to Dubai to work and earn money. Having worked for two years in Dubai, he returned with a little bit of money. He stayed back in Nepal and found a job in another migrant recruitment agency only to lose his job when the Government of Nepal temporarily banned recruitment of Nepali migrant workers to Malaysia, citing irregularities and exploitation of migrant workers. He was now working as an agent (*dalal*), sending migrant workers abroad.

Having moved to take up employment in cities like Kathmandu, village men and women went through a transformation. Employed women in Kathmandu showed more autonomy than their counterparts in the village, which was evident in their mobility for employment in the city. They were seen as part of a liberal environment, offered by city life, where they earned money and, in many cases, supported their family back home. A few women I met told me that they had a say in their choice of groom.

Most of the Bahun men I met during my fieldwork followed a radically different way of life from their counterparts back in the village. Several of them consumed alcohol, abandoned wearing *janai*,[3] visited cabin restaurants and dance bars,[4] ate momos[5] made from buffalo meat and started love affairs or married girls from a different caste. The Bahun men were under constant pressure to adopt a modern way of life, while, at the same time, they were conscious of their identity as a priestly caste. This was very much reflected in the consumption of alcohol among the employed Bahuns. One Bahun man (aged 31), employed as an accountant in a private firm, classified alcohol into two different types and told me that he drank branded beer or other branded liquor available in the shops, but did not drink *raksi*, the traditional local liquor. This pattern was quite common among many other employed Bahuns, who consumed branded alcohol (beer, wine, vodka, whisky, rum, wine and brandy), but did not consume the local alcohol (*raksi*). Those who drank branded alcohol did not call it *raksi*, but rather

3 Sacred thread; mainly worn by Bahuns and Chettris, it has symbolic importance for asserting ritual purity among Bahuns and Chettris.

4 People visiting the cabin restaurants and dance bars are looked down upon morally as it is believed that these function as brothels.

5 A popular meal in Kathmandu among the young and working people across different class background.

took the specific type or the name of the alcohol. To these Bahuns, branded alcohol, which they found easily in the city, but not in their village, was modern, but they kept themselves distant from *raksi*, as it was traditional alcohol consumed by the lower castes or other ethnic groups in their village. Most of these Bahuns did not drink alcohol when they went back to their village; neither did they consume alcohol when any family member or a close relative from the village visited them in the city. Except for a few, most of the young Bahuns told me that they did not like the idea of 'wearing the sacred thread' as they did not follow the strict ritual and discipline that they were supposed to observe in the village. One Bahun said, 'I think it is useless to wear the sacred thread here in Kathmandu. We eat in hotels; the food is cooked by anyone. We eat momo. It is not possible to live like a Bahun here. Nobody really cares.' Another Bahun told me that he did not like the idea of wearing the sacred thread, except for a few days after *janai purnima*,[6] as it often fell off his arm which led to humiliation. He preferred to take the sacred thread out in his wallet or keep it around his waist. He, and many others, told me that it was important to wear it when they went back home, especially during festivals and ceremonies, where it would be visible to others. Such strategic behaviour made it possible for them to adopt a modern way of life, without compromising their priestly identity. The Bahuns I met maintained a dual identity as liberal Bahuns in the city, while still maintaining their orthodox identity as a pure priestly caste back in the village. These employed Bahuns believed that it was important for them to change with the times, but still found it difficult to practise their liberal way of life when they visited their homes. In his paper on the commodification of food and sex among the middle class in Kathmandu, Liechty writes, 'Urban Nepalis shift between class bodies and caste bodies as they move through a varied cultural landscape in which different socio-

6 An annual religious festival when a new sacred thread is donned.

moral logics produce or demand different ways of being' (Liechty 2005, 4). He links the changing attitudes to alcohol and buffalo meat (in momos) among upper-caste men and the rise of public eating and restaurants in Kathmandu.

There was a Bahun man, who had married in the village, but it was rumoured that, after he went to Kathmandu to work, he had married another girl from a different caste. This form of freedom would have been almost impossible for him in the village. When I spoke to this man, who was teaching in a private boarding school in Kathmandu, he told me that he had met his new wife at his workplace and got married without informing his parents. He explained to me that, despite his insistence on marrying an educated girl with employment prospects, his parents, who wanted a daughter-in-law to help with household chores, had pressurised him into marrying his first wife. From his perspective, it was important to marry his new wife, who was educated and had a secure employment in the same school. Having a secure job enabled many men and women to make decisions about their life on their own and, in many cases, reject the social norms practised in the village.

In addition to pursuing and completing their education, the new place offered them a fresh network of friends and exposed them to different experiences in life. Those who went to colleges and universities experienced an unfamiliar political environment. Some of them took part in organisations and became politically active. This exposed them to new ideologies and aspirations, which again changed their relationship with home.

In Kathmandu, the Bahuns were more concerned about doing well in their jobs, earning money and adopting a modern way of life to enable them to climb the socio-economic ladder. Unlike Magars and other ethnic groups, the *jagire* Bahuns in Kathmandu were not organised as a collective group, except for some who took part in regional associations (for example, Palpali Sangam) or societies based on their *thar* (patronymic)—Gautam Samaj, Adhikari Samaj, Lamsal Samaj and others.

Responding to the anti-Bahun sentiment in the ethnic discourse in the university where he works, a Bahun lecturer in Kathmandu told me, 'I think Bahuns are being made scapegoats for nothing. People have invented the term *bahunism* (*bahunbad*). Now, some people are talking about a reservation system, like in India. I think it's time that Bahuns came together to do something about it. But Bahuns do not get along very well with each other.'

Bahuns coming to towns and cities became exposed to the discourses of ethnicity that categorised them as 'Bahuns', thus, developing their subjectivities as Bahuns. Unlike in the village where they were not exposed to the politicised identity of Bahuns, but practised rituals, they were now exposed to it at the same time, as they were giving up on their Bahun ritualistic identity. The politicised discourse on Bahuns had a powerful impact on Bahuns, who had begun to be aware of a different political moment. While the Bahuns had not developed an organised political movement in Kathmandu, there is an indication that young Bahuns have begun to find a political voice in the elite backlash against inclusion and state-restructuring.

The Magar men I met were conscious of their identity as Magars and took part in many of the Magar Association activities in Kathmandu. Almost all the employed Magars I met in Kathmandu were members of the Magar association and participated in the cultural and political activities organised by NEFIN. The Magar men I met in Kathmandu, who had invested in their educational, occupational and political futures in Nepal, did not see their future back in the village or in a foreign army. They were keen to complete their education and secure salaried jobs in the government, the booming NGO sector or the emerging private sector in Kathmandu. The Government of Nepal's inclusive policies and affirmative action meant that Magar men thought that they would find a place in the government jobs, from which they had historically been excluded.

Dalit men faced discrimination and rejection in the city as soon as they arrived. Upper-caste landlords in Kathmandu and Tansen did not rent out their rooms to Dalits. As the upper-caste landlords asked for their surname or caste (*thar*), they either had to hide their Dalit caste try to secure accommodation or risk being rejected. Either way, Dalit young men's first encounter with the city made them realise that caste was as important in the city as it was in the village. Many Dalit men changed their surnames as a way to avoid being overtly discriminated against in the city. All the Dalit men I met in Tansen and Kathmandu had difficulty securing accommodation. While the Dalit men did not experience overt forms of discrimination in the educational spaces, they soon realised that they did not have the social and political networks or confidence that some of their upper-caste friends had. They were aware of the discourses of inclusion and affirmative action, and they had begun to see their future in the city as they sought to secure salaried jobs. Dalit men had started to find salaried jobs in the city, particularly in the NGO sector, and a few had become successful in securing government jobs. Many felt that they had experienced covert forms of discrimination at the workplace, including upper-caste colleagues not sharing food or rooms while travelling. In the evolving political context, Dalit men in the city had to walk a delicate balance between not disclosing their caste identity to avoid overt discrimination and disclosing their caste identity to secure the benefits that came with affirmative action and inclusive policies.

Emerging Caste and Ethnic Identities in Cities

Rural young men face significant challenges as they navigate their educational and occupational futures in the city. As sites of opportunity for education, jobs and politics, cities and towns offer participation in modernity and broader networks and connect the youth to new, potentially lucrative opportunities in the wider world. However, moving to town may devalue young people's rural identity and leave them with unmet aspirations and the lack of social mobility. Yet, as discussed in this chapter, while ideas of modernity shape Nepali young men's mobility to the city, relocation to the city at a moment of intense state restructuring creates new forms of ethnic and caste consciousness. The process of how this occurred for upper-caste Bahuns, Adivasi Janajati Magars and former-untouchable Dalits was markedly different.

As Bahun men arrived in the city and began socialisation in 'modern' life, whereby, they gave up certain aspects of their priestly Bahun identity, such as no longer wearing the sacred thread, eating buffalo meat, drinking alcohol or visiting dance bars, which would have been forbidden in the village, the process of relocating to the city paradoxically made their Bahun identity more visible, as they were seen by others as historically privileged Bahuns. The context for this social construction of identity by 'others' was mainly shaped by the intense debates and discourses on social exclusion and state-restructuring in Nepal. Consequently, Bahun men were conscious of the public discourses on historical privilege that came to be associated with their caste heritage. Yet, poor rural Bahun men who struggled to secure salaried jobs in the city found it difficult to accept these discourses on historical privilege. Their mobility to the city had meant that young Bahun men were less Bahun in terms of the Bahun rituals, but had come to be viewed as Bahuns by others, thus, shaping their consciousness as an ethnic group (Daryn 2003). While Bahun men had not formed a political or ethnic organisation, unlike their Adivasi Janajati counterparts, there are signs of upper-caste resentment against the progressive policies on social inclusion and affirmative action adopted by the Nepali state. It is possible that young Bahun men, particularly those without the social and political networks required to secure educational and occupational futures in the city, may see their sentiments reflected in a countermovement against affirmative action.

Magar men's mobility to the city gave Magar men, from different parts of the country, the chance to come together under the umbrella of Magar associations or cultural activities in Tansen or Kathmandu, or loose networks of Magars, and this was instrumental in Magar ethnic consciousness. As Magar men came in contact with Magar associations and got exposed to a particular exclusionary history of the Nepali state, young Magars from different parts of Nepal identified themselves as a single ethnic group called Magars, and also as Adivasi Janajatis, together with several other ethnic groups. Again, there was a paradoxical process of identity formation here. Magar men who came to the city began to reassert and rediscover their cultural practices in the process of becoming Magars. Some Magar men who had been identifying themselves as Hindu stopped calling themselves Hindu, stopped wearing tika in the Hindu festival of Dashain and formed broader solidarity with other Adivasi Janajati groups.

Dalit young men's experience of the city was markedly different from that of Bahuns and Magars. Not only was their rural Dalit identity devalued in the city, unlike that of the Bahuns or Magars, they also had very few social and political networks or associational life to help them survive and thrive in towns. Critically, Dalits were reminded of their 'untouchable' identity as they searched for their rental accommodation (*dera*) or faced covert forms of discrimination in the workplace. The Dalit men I met were aware of the public debates and discourses on their historical marginalisation and the process of inclusionary state-restructuring that was underway and felt that, in theory, there was increased opportunity for education and jobs. Nonetheless, getting into those spaces required social and political networks as well as confidence, which poorer Dalit men lacked.

Overall, not only were young men from different castes, classes and ethnicities differently equipped to navigate opportunities in the city, their mobility at the precise time of state-restructuring profoundly affected their ethnic, caste and gender identity. Further, deeper investigation is needed to understand the impact of state-restructuring on the educational and occupational futures of young men and women from different castes and ethnicities. This chapter has focused on the experiences of young men; focused investigation and analysis are needed on the gendered perceptions, aspirations and experiences of rural women from different castes, classes and ethnicities who travel to the city in search of a future.

References

Adhikari, K.R. 1993. 'The Participation of the Magars in Nepalese Development'. PhD diss. Texas: University of Austin.

Daryn, G. 2003. 'Bahuns: Ethnicity without and "Ethnic Group"'. In *Ethnic Revival and Religious Turmoil: Identities and Representations in the Himalayas*, edited by Lecomte-Tilouine and P. Dollfus, 162–173. New Delhi: Oxford University Press.

Des Chene, M.K. 1991. 'Relics of Empire: A Cultural History of the Gurkhas 1815–1987'. PhD diss. Stanford: Stanford University.

Liechty, M. 2005. 'Carnal Economies: The Commodification of Food and Sex in Kathmandu'. *Cultural Anthropology*, 20(1), 1–38.

Pigg, S.L. 1992. 'Inventing Social Categories through Place—Social Representations and Development in Nepal'. *Comparative Studies in Society and History*, 34: 491–513.

Sharma, J.R. 2019. *Crossing the Border to India: Youth, Migration and Masculinities in Nepal*. New Delhi: Bloomsbury.

Stash, S., and E. Hannum. 2001. 'Who Goes to School? Educational Stratification by Gender, Caste, and Ethnicity in Nepal'. *Comparative Education Review*, 45(3), 354–378.

A large part of the development budget spent constructing roads connecting remote villages to market towns, cities and highways, road connecting Rolpa from Dang, 2009.

5

Development and Patronage Politics

Introduction

Starting from the 1950s, development policies and programmes, supported by foreign aid, have penetrated all the aspects of Nepali citizens' lives. Through its ideology, social and political networks, and mobilisation of expertise, financial and material resources, development pursued by the post-1950 Nepali state, which has come to be known as *bikas* by the public, has shaped every aspect of the society, politics and economy of Nepal. Indeed, it is virtually impossible to find any feature of life and livelihoods in rural Nepal that is not touched by ideas and materials of development, ranging from schools and hospitals, land, agriculture, roads, bridges, dams, family, childhood, youth, elderly and gender, to administrative systems and training of bureaucrats, among others.

The disjuncture between the promises of development, expressed as policies and programmes, and the reality of poor outcomes has been a major issue of concern for social scientists and policymakers. Nepal's struggle for development has produced a considerable body of analyses and critiques. Here, it is useful to look at a couple of indicative texts to illustrate two main attempts at explaining this gap between the intention and the outcomes of development. On the one hand, there are critiques of development by scholars, like Nanda R. Shrestha, who argue that development has not only created colonial-like hierarchies, but also produced development victims (Shrestha 1998). On the other hand, there are other writings that focus on the evaluative assessment of development, primarily within the state-framing of development, whether its conclusions are more critical (Pandey 1999), or more hopeful (Mahat 2020). While the former appears to be so ideologically driven that it fails to even consider any possibility of change through development and the latter exclusively views development from the vantage point of a rational policy framework that does not allow the examination of unintended consequences outside the framing of the policy.

The dividing scholarship on Nepal's tryst with development mirrors David Mosse's assessment that the debate on development has been constrained by two opposing views on development policy (Mosse 2005). First, there are critical perspectives that treat development as politics by domination and see failure as self-evident. Second, there are instrumental perspectives that view policy as a rational problem-solving instrument, but completely ignore the politics that undergirds development. For the latter, the lack of development has meant the need for more development or for making development more effective through deregulation, new forms of managerialisms and technical interventions such as results-based programming. Not only have these opposing instrumental and critical views blocked the way for a more insightful ethnography of development capable of opening up the implementation black box (Mosse 2005, 5), they also ignore the institutional processes and the role of actors, that is, how the delivery of aid and global development policies are mediated through several actors, institutions and arrangements (Lewis and Mosse 2006). Understanding the space between the lofty objectives of development and its poor outcomes requires analytical attention to the actual practices by assessing actors and institutions, both formal and informal, rather than to the intention of development.

Development not only provides new streams of income, and exercise of power and patronage, but also offers new cosmopolitan discourses that generate different understandings on the ground, and introduce vocabularies of promises, new logics, awareness and ideologies. Large amounts of resources flow through various development institutions, often involving a range of brokers and intermediaries. Resource-flow, including how money travels and gets distributed, in the form of projects, jobs and contracts, remain fundamental questions. Development is also a part of transnational networks that are not only geographically extensive and tie global institutions, ideas, discourses and professionals to national and local places, but also institutional in that they link various international, national, local, governmental, non-governmental, for-profit and non-profit institutions, disciplines, technology frameworks, knowledge systems and professionals. Moreover, development does not take place on a blank slate; it operates in an unequal field and a field that is marred by historical legacies and political interests.

Nepal's encounter with development has received extensive attention from scholars. Several scholars have offered useful insights on the history of development, including the history of capitalist development, planned development during the Panchayat era and the ubiquitous role of foreign aid in Nepal (Mihaly 1965, Gyawali 2017, Sharma 2001, Skerry et al. 1991, Pandey 1999, Mishra 1987, Khadka 1997, Dixit 1997, Blaikie et al. 1980, Sharma and Harper 2018, Gyawali et al. 2017). Likewise, anthropologists working on Nepal have offered various insights on the intended and unintended consequences of development, including discourses on the disjuncture between policies and outcomes (Pigg 1993, Fujikura 2013, Harper 2014, Stone 1989, Justice 1986, Sharma 2008). What has been less often attempted in the context of Nepal is a complex historical understanding of the multiple facets of and the way in which ideas and materiality of development activities have affected Nepali society, politics and economy.

So, what are the political and economic effects of planned development, and how has planned development intersected with the formal and informal political economy? This chapter reflects on Nepal's planned development journey and the challenges encountered when enmeshed within the context of power, patronage and politics. Unlike the Shah and Rana eras, where the rich thrived on the extraction of rent from peasants, the planned development post-1950 was associated with the idea of distributing welfare and public goods. In this context, this chapter explores the consequences of this shift in distributive politics. It examines how the idea of development as distribution has, in fact, not only created new citizens, but also created vulnerabilities through distributional coalitions that are firmly rooted in clientelism and patronage politics in Nepal. This chapter focuses on the real politics of development, that is, it focuses on how things are done rather than how things ought to be done. Thus, the chapter emphasises on the actual practice of carrying out development. The purpose of this chapter is not to offer an evaluative assessment of development in Nepal in a traditional sense of the term, but examine how development has shaped the nature and form of Nepal's political economy.

The next sections offer a history of development and foreign aid in Nepal, organised under various political regimes.

Political History of Development

Unlike in India, where historians have extensively documented precolonial and colonial development processes and strategies, the scholarship on Nepal's development history mostly takes 1950 as the starting point. The dominant view sees pre-1950 Nepal as a dark age and a blank slate, but overlooks how institutional legacies have impacted and influenced the post-1950s quest for development (Gyawali 2017). First, such an ahistorical framing closely resonates with the idea of imaging Nepal as a timeless and isolated Shangri-la, discovered by the outside world only after 1950 (Lietchty 2017). In his popular treatise, *Imagining India*, Ronald Inden argues how the colonial ethnography on India tends to represent the country as a land of self-contained and inward-turned villages, consisting of cooperative agents (Inden 1990). According to him, the politics of discourse on the construction of Indian villages is to displace a complex polity with an ancient India and appropriate it as an external member of modern Britain (Inden 1990). Inden argues that these representations must be viewed as knowledge produced by 'others' through their dominance, which undermines human agency (Inden 1990). Second, this way of conceiving the pre-1950s as the dark age of Nepal's history is a part of its nationalist history that has directly or indirectly sought to justify and legitimise the post-1950 regime as a progressive one that seeks to break away from the feudal and extractive image of the past. Third, such an association of development with the post-1950s is directly influenced by the discourses and debates on foreign aid and theories of international development, where the history of development starts with modernisation and foreign aid, following the Second World War and the reconstruction of the world and decolonisation. Accordingly, US President Truman's Four Point Program and flow of aid are seen as the starting point of development in developing countries.

Yet, it would be wrong to say that there was no thought of planned development prior to 1950 in Nepal. Evidence shows that planning for development was an agenda during the Rana regime. Just before the Second World War, the government had announced a 20-year plan, but nothing was done about it. Again, when Mohan Shamsher Rana was the prime minister, towards the end of Rana rule, Nepal set up a National Planning Committee tasked with preparing a 15-year economic development plan to make Nepal self-sufficient. The plan had the following features (Pant 1956):

1. Expansion of agricultural production
2. Cultivation of indigenous herbs and plants in the plains
3. Development of medium-sized and cottage industries for exports
4. Improvement in means of transport and communications

Gyawali (2018) offers a number of examples of programmes undertaken during the Rana era that would fall under what is broadly regarded as development. Six students were sent to Japan for technical training in 1902. There was a ropeway for transporting goods, said to have been conceived as early as 1904, but eventually built in 1924, over the Mahabharata Range, southwest of Kathmandu, connecting Kathmandu to the town of Bhimphedi. This 14-mile-long ropeway was built at the cost of £100,000 and supplied by London-based contractors. A 29-mile-long railway line was built in 1927, connecting the Indian border town of Raxaul to the town of Amlekhgunj in Nepal. A 28-mile motorable road was built from Amlekhgunj to the town of Bhimphedi, connecting India to Kathmandu. A hydroelectric station was installed just outside Kathmandu in Pharping in 1911. Tri-Chandra College was set up in 1918. Slavery was abolished in Nepal in 1925. The Janakpur (Nepal)–Jayanagar (India) railway was constructed in 1940. There were new road networks in Kathmandu, a limited number of telephone lines and a few educational institutions that were enjoyed by the ruling elite. Several industries were set up in the Terai with joint investments from the Rana elite and the Indian Marwari community. Although the primary motivation for undertaking these activities is said to have been the Rana rulers' desire to personally benefit from the improvements, the legacy of these interventions, both in terms of their material presence as well as political intentions, continue to shape the development trajectories in Nepal.

Despite all these initiatives, it is useful to look at 1950 as a critical moment in Nepal's development history for a number of reasons.

First, unlike the Shah and Rana eras where the state was considered to be extractive, the state in 1950 presented itself as a distributive state, one that distributes welfare and other benefits to its citizens. Not only did the state designate former subjects as citizens, but it also saw its duty to develop and modernise society through the distribution of public goods in the name of development.

Second, the post-1950 Nepali state sought legitimacy and authority through development. Indeed, development became the raison d'être of the Nepali state. Development has been a justification for the existence of the Nepali state, its policies, institutions and politics. Despite regime changes and specific politics attached to it, development remained a central feature of the state during the Panchayat era, the multiparty democracy, the Maoist insurgency and when Nepal transformed into a secular, federal and republican state. From manifestos of political parties and the ruling elite to the demands of social and political movements, developmental narratives have been all-pervasive.

Third, 1950 saw the entry of foreign aid into Nepal, which made a fundamental change in how development was viewed, funded and practised. Nepal's political transition was not accidental; it coincided with a new liberal order in international politics. Foreign aid was designed to assist former colonies, now called the Third World, and the UN system was designed to support development based on solidarity. Nepal tapped directly into this new liberal order of international development. The presence of bilateral donors and, later, multilateral donors, have played a key role in Nepal's development.

Fourth, along with foreign aid came planning and expertise that defined the norms and forms of development for the decades to come. The centralised planning meant that there was very little understanding of the local context. The planners had very little knowledge of the countryside or the local people's willingness or ability to take advantage of the programmes, creating significant gaps between policies and practices (Justice 1986).

For all these reasons, foreign aid has been the subject of the development rhetoric in Nepal and a crucial part of Nepal's development experience, and its successes and failures.

1950–1960: Nepal's Initial Rush for Development in the New Era

After the end of the Rana era, Nepal entered a period of democratisation for a decade between 1951 and 1960, before the royal coup that introduced the Panchayat system in December 1960. Politically, this period was qualitatively different from the Rana and Shah regimes and aspirations for development and modernisation were apparent. In a sharp departure from tradition, King Tribhuwan on 17 February 1951 addressed the nation as 'beloved people' as opposed to 'the notables of the land' (Riaz and Basu 2008, 99).

A major defining feature in this decade was the entry of foreign aid, and with it came not only financial resources, but also expertise and effort to produce statistical and other data on the country's development (Mihaly 1965, Skerry et al. 1991). Indeed, foreign aid came into the country in 1951 and shaped development priorities before there had been any serious thinking on planned development within Nepal (Adhikari 2014, Pandey 1999). Foreign aid made its official debut into Nepal with the signing of the Four Point agreement with the United States on 23 January 1951, followed by aid from India and China (Mihaly 1965). Designed within the modernisation framework of 'diffusion of innovation', the US mission's first initiative was a 'Village Development Project' that started by setting up a training centre in Kathmandu to train men in agricultural technology. In turn, the trainees were expected to disseminate these skills to village communities through satellite centres (Fujikura 2013). The US was a major donor that played a key role in malaria eradication and promoted road construction and the introduction of technology. A written account by administrator Paul Rose explains the motivation of the USOM (the United States Operations Mission, a former avatar of the USAID) in providing this support and sets the tone for the US approach to Nepal's needs. Historian Tom Robertson quotes Rose and offers some insightful observations in his article titled 'DDT and the Cold War Jungle: American Environmental and Social Engineering in the Rapti Valley of Nepal':

> Because no motorable road reached out of the Kathmandu Valley, Rose and his group ventured out of Nepal's capital by the only means available: on foot. Starting at 4,200 feet in elevation, Rose and his group hiked a dirt trail over a seven-thousand-foot pass, then dropped

> to the plains. On the far side of the pass, Rose stepped into a scene that brought into sharp focus his vision of development for Nepal: a group of men struggling to get an automobile up the mountain trail. The men were not driving or pushing the car; they were carrying it. Rose counted ninety barefoot, ill-clad porters: sixty shouldering the bamboo poles supporting the vehicle, and thirty pulling from above with a rope. The scene was not unusual for Nepal. Many of Kathmandu's supplies—and indeed most wealthy Kathmanduites who journeyed to and from India—were carried.
>
> For Rose, the situation revealed Nepal's core problems. Here was a country that, it seemed, literally lacked the wheel. Ordinary life involved little or no technology. But the man-carrying-car spectacle also revealed another crucial fact: the country's vast political and economic disparities. While a tiny elite could purchase vehicles to carry themselves and their goods, the majority hauled the loads of others. Their plight deeply moved Rose. (2018, 911)

He adds:

> Assessing the valley's uncultivated land, Rose blamed not just malaria but also the Rana aristocrats who had run Nepal for their own benefit. The old regime had monopolized the valley's resources for private enjoyment as a hunting ground, to the detriment of the greater good. While ordinary Nepalis were dirt poor, the ruling elite had hoarded resources to pursue decadent pastimes. To open resources for all Nepalis, Rose stressed two technological initiatives: road building and malaria control. (Robertson 2018, 913)

The US has continued to play a central role in shaping Nepal's development programmes; its presence and legacy are found in almost every single aspect of development in Nepal, including community development, agriculture, road construction, health, family planning, education and human resources, among many others (Skerry et al. 1991). In my interviews, retired and current bureaucrats, planners and development professionals recall the intense engagement of the US in Nepal's development since 1950.

In this first decade, aid from different countries began to trickle in countries, such as the US, India and China, competed for geopolitical influence. While the primary motivation for US assistance was said to be strengthening countries and governments vulnerable to the threat of communism, aid from India and China, as Nepal's immediate neighbours with opposing ideologies, focused on strategic sectors, such as road building and airport construction. The first two major projects undertaken by India were an airport in Kathmandu and a road linking Kathmandu to the Indian border town of Raxaul (Adhikari 2014).

After Nepal joined the United Nations in 1955 and the Colombo Plan in 1956, multilateral agencies started to provide assistance in the form of grants and loans. Aid from India and the United States was followed by aid from the United Kingdom, Switzerland and China, and later by Norway and Japan during the 1960s. British aid did not feature prominently in Nepal, and its support was limited to fellowships for Nepalis under the Colombo plan, material support in the form of donation of motorcycles to the Nepal Army in 1950 and a 70-bed British Military Hospital at the Gorkha recruitment centre in Dharan in 1957, primarily to service the medical needs of Gorkha soldiers serving in the British Army and their families (Nickson 1992, Sharma and Harper 2018).

Emerging from the Rana rule, from the perspective of planners, there were at least three major challenges: the lack of knowledge and statistical data on development needs, the lack of administrative and technical expertise and the lack of financial resources (Pant 1956). The urge for modernisation was reflected in the initial institutional undertakings, such as the establishment of the Ministry of Planning and Public Works, which was renamed the Ministry of Planning and Development in 1955. On 10 October 1955, a Royal proclamation was issued by King Mahendra announcing a Five-year Plan for Nepal for attaining self-sufficiency. The Planning Commission was established in 1958, and the Central Bureau of Statistics was set up in 1959, which paved the way for planned development and the employment of experts.

In the first decade, politicians, planners and aid workers stationed in Nepal were clear that Nepal's agricultural development required not just diffusion of technology, but also addressing historical inequalities through the politically difficult issue of land reform. As indicated above, this was reflected in Paul Rose's observations. In the same article, Robertson (2018) writes that the US Ambassador to Nepal, Chester Bowles, wrote to Tribhuwan as early as 1953 '[Nepal's people] have become more aware that modern science and technology can enable them to overcome the threat of malaria, to open up inaccessible mountain valleys, to harness the streams for electric power, increase the yield of human labor many times over, and to secure a more fair return for their labor.'

The political changes in 1950 had a profound impact on the land ownership policy. The interim constitution declared the right to acquire, use and sell property to be a fundamental one (Regmi 1977). The call for land reform gained political momentum with Nepal's political parties raising the question of inequality and land as early as 1951. There were peasant movements calling for land reform, including the formation of the All Nepal Peasants Association in 1952. The Royal Land Reform Commission was established in 1952. The Nepal Communist Party called for the confiscation of land and its distribution to tenants and landless people, while the Nepali Congress party adopted a very popular slogan '*Jamin jotneko, ghar potne ko* (land belongs to the tiller, house belongs to the painter)'. The 1957 Land Act and the 1959 Birta Abolition Act were adopted in an attempt to address land reform by granting security to tenants. However, these reforms were hardly implemented as the landholding class still had a grip on power. Many in the political class were also landed class, resulting in a disjuncture between the political rhetoric of land reform and a lack of political commitment to implement it in practice (Regmi 1977).

1961–1990: Panchayat System—Nation-Building through *Bikas*

In December 1960, when King Mahendra took over through a coup and introduced the Panchayat system, a partyless, centralised political system, run by an absolute monarch, development became a central part of a new regime that lasted for three decades before being replaced by multiparty democracy in 1990. The two key features of the Panchayat system were to pursue a partyless, centralised political system, and mobilise Nepal's rural population in the pursuit of national development under the ideology of *bikas* and modernisation. King Mahendra systematically manipulated development and foreign aid to consolidate his rule and the Panchayat system (Sharma and Harper 2018). The Nepali word *bikas* became a key political discourse in this modernising project (Pigg 1992, Gyawali 2017).

The Panchayat system's fundamental philosophy was 'development first and democracy second' (Khadka 1991). In other words, King Mahendra promoted *bikas* as a prerequisite for democracy. His son, King Birendra, continued with this policy of Panchayat for development. King Mahendra in his proclamation had declared that his vision of basic democracy under Panchayat would open up a 'new spring of power, which will remove the centuries-old poverty, ignorance and backwardness of the country' and pursue this dream through the institution of Panchayat at different levels, that is, from the village, district and national levels (Khadka 1991, 696). The king's slogans, repeated on the radio and in newspapers, as well as in public places, emphasised on the need for *bikas*.

By design or default, the governance structure of Panchayat helped maintain and even strengthen patronage networks. The Panchayat had several layers of elected assemblies. The lowest level was the village Panchayat, some 4,000 of them throughout Nepal, which linked several villages into an assembly led by a chairman.

Each village Panchayat chairman was a member of the District-wide Panchayat, which elected a chairman for the District Panchayat in all 75 districts. One or two representatives were directly elected at the Rastriya Panchayat or National Assembly at the centre. The king directly appointed about 28 of the National Panchayat members to represent what was called *bargiya sangathan* or class organisations. Such appointments gave the king a firm control over the National Assembly. The formation of the cabinet and the election of the prime minister took place with the king's support. Such a system of representation and the banning of political parties meant that the king could avoid any threat of opposition to his rule. The lack of political parties also meant that the traditional elite and landed classes could continue to maintain their dominance in the Panchayat system at village, district and national levels. The structure maintained the pattern of patron-client relationships that had existed in Rana Nepal; a village leader would have to align himself with the district leader to obtain development projects and monies (Metz 1995, 177–178). The landed class and upper caste, through their economic and political networks, such as *chakari* and *aafno manche*, strengthened their key positions in politics, business and the bureaucracy. The ability to secure positions in the Panchayat and bureaucracy gave the upper caste and landed class access to government funds and the chance to siphon money into their own pockets.

Land reform was considered to be of critical importance in the successful implementation of the economic and political goals of the Panchayat system. Between 1964 and 1966, a comprehensive land reform programme was introduced. Broadly speaking, this focused on: a ceiling on land ownership and tenancy holdings, security of tenancy rights, rent control by fixing it at a maximum of 50 per cent of the main crop, agrarian reform by encouraging shift labour and capital from the agricultural to the non-agricultural sectors and introduction of compulsory savings and credits provisions.

Despite these progressive policies on land reform, the government gave ample time to the landed class to distribute their holdings among relatives to avoid confiscation of land under the land-ceiling policy. The policy on land ceiling, therefore, remained political rhetoric. Moreover, these policies had negative consequences for peasants. Despite the offer of low-interest rates, getting loans from the government and paying back the loan in cash was not easy. The requirement to pay tax in cash meant that people had to sell their agricultural produce in the market and migrate to earn some cash income.

While land reform policies were radical, they had little impact on the agrarian structures. The reform is said to have strengthened the landowners' position as rent receivers without any obligations beyond collecting rents after the crops had been harvested (Regmi 1977). Overall, the fact that the landed class and upper-caste groups held administrative and political positions meant no real change in the agrarian systems. Instead, the reforms protected the landed class, many of whom were politicians or bureaucrats in the Panchayat system. The king and the Panchayat system survived on the loyalty of these patronage networks; thus, there was no political pressure to modify the old system.

Although the policies and institutions that came with *bikas* were new and distributional in rhetoric, the transformation of 1950 did not necessarily lead to transformation in the character of the Nepali state's bureaucracy or its caste-based patronage system. Despite formal legal changes that did not discriminate based on caste, ethnicity or gender, high caste men's dominance continued in education and state bureaucracy. The old landlords continued to exert power through former patronage networks. The new bureaucrats came from high castes and were male. The practice of *chakari* continued to flourish during the rule. It was men from the upper castes and landed classes that occupied the palace secretariat, army and bureaucracy during the Panchayat system. In 1967, 73 per cent of the National Assembly members were from high castes; by 1980, this proportion had increased to nearly 78 per cent (Levine 1987).

In these decades, the push for agricultural development without real agrarian change and land reform had a minimal impact on rural poverty. As they did not address the structural constraints, the development projects that attempted technocratic solutions did not result in increased productivity or equitable distribution of rent. King Mahendra mobilised support from donors for road construction, and investments were made primarily in the East-West highway and roads connecting Kathmandu to district headquarters, which served the king's purpose by strengthening his control. In the east, Britain funded a road, linking the Indian border town of Jogbini to Dharan, which was later extended to Dhankuta, Hille and Basantapur in the hills. Britain also supported a part of King Mahendra's East-West highway project between Narayangadh and Butwal and upgrading of the Mugling–Malekhu section of the road connecting Kathmandu to Pokhara and Narayangath (Sharma and Harper 2018). Likewise, the widespread promotion of schooling in the Nepali language helped drive King Mahendra's vision of Nepali nationalism through a one-nation, one-language policy. During the Panchayat period, the inauguration ceremonies of development projects instilled a sense of shared Nepali nationhood, and the government officials replaced the old non-Nepali place names with Nepali-sounding names (Adhikari 1996).

Britain also funded Radio Nepal by providing studio equipment, with a 100 KW medium wave and a 100 KW short wave transmitter. It also helped set up Buddhanilkantha School, an elite school in the outskirts of Kathmandu, as a part of its nation-building project. British aid provided machinery, presses and other printing equipment to the Ministry of Information and the state-controlled newspaper, *Gorkhapatra*, which were key instruments through which the Panchayat regime promoted its version of nationalism (Nickson 1992). While literacy programmes were promoted, they were limited to functional literacy. Family planning and health programmes were promoted as a way to control population growth. The eradication of malaria through DDT-spray programmes, supported by the USAID and WHO, enabled the resettlement of the hill population in the Terai, which again fitted with King Mahendra's nationalist policy in the Terai. All of these development strategies helped the Panchayat to maintain its centralised state power and prevented the possibility of dissent through strict administrative measures and surveillance. Foreign aid was a key factor that significantly legitimised and helped consolidate the Panchayat system. During the Panchayat era, aid was channelled through the state apparatus, and there was control over the civil society groups and NGOs that helped the Panchayat government monopolise and manipulate aid. There was a limited presence of NGOs, and they were regulated through the Social Service National Coordination Council (SSNCC), which was chaired by the queen. Limited attempts at industrialisation did not create the required jobs. Indeed, the development strategy during the Panchayat period did not focus on generating employment. Due to subsistence agriculture, the economy remained stagnant.

The survival of the Panchayat regime largely depended on a flow of foreign aid that did not require any public accountability from Nepali citizens. This uninterrupted flow of foreign aid meant that King Mahendra could survive without raising significant revenue domestically. 'While the earlier tribute-extracting patrimonial state of the Rana regime siphoned resources from countryside into the urban metropolis of Kathmandu in alliance with rural landed elements, the new monarchical regime appropriated foreign aid provided by external donors within the limits of capitals' urban environments' (Riaz and Basu 2008, 98–99). Informed by global discourse, Nepal's 5th plan for the first time talked about growth distribution. Meeting basic needs was the slogan in the 6th and 7th plans and, by the 1980s, this had become a political slogan for the Panchayat (Khadka 1991). King Birendra, who took the throne in 1972, promoted the idea of *bikas ko mul phutao* (let the spring of development open).

In the 1980s, there was sluggish growth, stagnant exports and an import-led macroeconomic crisis, including a balance of payments crisis. Like many other developing countries, the government, on the advice of the International Monetary Fund (IMF) and the World Bank (WB), launched a series of reforms for short-term economic stabilisation and longer-term structural adjustment. Accordingly, the Nepali Rupee was devalued, import regimes were liberalised, the industrial licensing system was eased and export procedures simplified. These reforms were further intensified after the restoration of democracy and the Nepali Congress coming to power in the early 1990s (Mahat 2020).

Overall, during the Panchayat era, development, supported by foreign aid, worked to maintain the regime's grip on power.

1990–1996: Democratisation for Development

1990 heralded a new era in Nepal's development. In the people's movement of 1990, Nepal's political parties fought to bring freedom, democracy and development. The restoration of democracy and adoption of a new constitution was significant because it opened up the possibility of an accountable political culture that could address widespread poverty and inequality. The new constitution of 1991 guaranteed fundamental rights and imagined a society that was beyond the narrow patronage sustained by the monarchy. The new era of multiparty democracy, represented by different political parties, was to institutionalise democracy for development. Unlike the Panchayat system, that saw development first and democracy second, the new political system saw democratisation as a critical force for development. In this new era, development was conceived in terms of democracy and freedom. With the restoration of democracy, there was a widespread aspiration for socio-economic development.

The king's role was now limited to being a constitutional monarch, although the king continued to wield power in the new political system through the loyalty of the Nepal Army, as well as through deeply rooted patronage networks in the bureaucracy, judiciary and political parties.

In the new multiparty democracy, unlike the Panchayat system, various political parties with different ideologies contested the local and national elections. Development remained the key rhetoric in the manifestos of political parties. One of the principal changes in the new political system was to get rid of the nomenclature of Panchayat. For example, 'Village Panchayats' were replaced by 'Village Development Committees' (VDCs) and 'District Panchayats' (DDCs) were replaced by 'District Development Committees', although little changed in the operation of these institutions. Elections were held at national and local levels. At the national level, Nepal was divided into 205 single-member constituencies, each of which elected one member of parliament (MP). Citizens of 18 years of age and above would directly elect their MP for a term of five years. Additionally, the national assembly had 60 MPs, 35 elected by the House of Representatives, 15 from 5 development regions and 10 appointed by the king. At the local level, each VDC contained 9 wards, and a municipality consisted of 9 to 35 wards. The election of these local bodies was held in 1992, and again in 1997. The enactment of the Local Self-Governance Act (LSGA) in 1999 expanded the mandates of local bodies, devolving the powers, responsibilities and resources. However, the election of local bodies did not happen after the introduction of LSGA. Nonetheless, local democracy began to take root in the 1990s.

Development remained the central part of the Nepali state's mission, but the vision was different. Within the democratisation framework, there was a push for participation, decentralisation and local democracy of development. This approach was a significant change in how disbursement for development was made, whereby, the local bodies and politicians could decide how to spend the money.

When the UML government gained power in 1994 for nine months, it adopted a popular programme called *aano gaau aafnai banau* (build your village on your own), where a set budget of Nepali rupees, ₹300,000, was allocated for spending by each VDC. Each electoral constituency was allocated ₹250,000 in the half-year's budget. Over the years, as we will discuss later in this chapter, this particular modality of funding for development has mutated and expanded exponentially into millions of Nepali rupees, under the respective banners of individual Member of Parliament Development Fund, Constituency Development Fund and, more recently, the Local Infrastructure Partnership Programme. Despite the stated purpose of enhancing local people's participation, such funds' transparency and accountability have been a concern. Pfaff-Czarnecka's accounts from her study in the Bajhang district in far western Nepal show how these development resources began instituting 'distributional coalitions', enabling political elites across political parties to siphon off resources consensually. Voters meanwhile were unable to stop their representatives from joining distributional coalitions even though their activities were detrimental to voters (Pfaff-Czarnecka 2008).

The transition to democracy in 1990 also involved a significant transition to neoliberal development. More specifically, space for development opened for other actors apart from the State. The State was not the sole actor for development, and space opened up for NGOs and private actors.

After 1990, the SSNCC was replaced by the Social Welfare Council, and NGOs could now obtain funds from international partners. The interim government encouraged international and local NGOs to work on development and made it easier for the NGOs to attract foreign funding. Many political activists, especially from the Left, started NGOs and human rights organisations. The 8th (1992–1997) and 9th (1997–2002) five-year plans highlighted the role of NGOs in development. Both the government and the international development community saw NGOs as a vehicle for development.

Within 16 years (between 1990 and 2006), the number of NGOs in Nepal had expanded from 193 to 33,000 (Shah, 2008). This change offered lucrative employment opportunities for the emergent middle class. Political activists, critical voices and intellectuals were absorbed by the NGO industry (Ismail 2017).

A significant development during this period was the growth of community-based organisations, user groups and local committees supported by NGOs and development organisations, ushering in a new era of grassroots democracy and development. In theory, group-based social mobilisation enables women, the poor and the excluded to take part in the public sphere and to make claims on rights and resources. The 'imaginary' of egalitarianism within development groups generates not just economic and social capital within the group, but also collective consciousness and resistance to oppression (Shah 2018). In his study of women's groups supported by a follow-on[1] to the government's Production Credit for Rural Women (PCRW) project in central Nepal, Saubhgya Shah found that women did not just participate in the economic and agricultural programmes of the project, but they also used the forum to initiate activities related to women's concerns, namely, securing property rights for women, checking domestic violence, gaining political representation and controlling gambling and alcoholism. He found that beyond the FAO's (Food and Agricultural Organisation's) intention, the women's group (*mahila karyakari*) had evolved into an entity with an autonomous will that started taking up issues: getting women a share in their husband's property when they were abandoned; intervening in cases of domestic violence and abuse against women; challenging the practices of polygyny and child marriage; banning gambling by men and working to gain women's representation in local municipal governance (Shah 2018).

1 This follow-on project entitled 'Enhancing the Agricultural Production Capacity of Rural Women' was funded by FAO and implemented by the Women's Development Division

However, these dynamics are shaped by the local political economy in which they operate, and such local groups can also end up reproducing existing hierarchies. Building on her work on traditional *guthi*s and micro-credit institutions in Nepal, Katharine Rankin has argued that generating social capital through *guthi* obligations entails significant costs that can undermine both commercial initiatives and social transformation (Rankin 2004). Her work shows that as caste-based associations, *guthi*s exclude outsiders, notably the lower castes and women, and play a key role in regulating the social hierarchy. The benefits from the development groups are not always evenly distributed, with some individuals and groups excluded or unable to participate, and others participating in a formalistic way, but with no, or even negative, returns. Because development activities bring power and resources, they become a site of struggle for control that excludes some, while including others.

Importantly, 1990 was also characterised by the intensification of structural adjustment programmes imposed by the WB and IMF in the mid-1980s. While much of the content of the 8th plan was a continuation of the 7th plan, the 8th plan articulated a shift in the development paradigm. It stated that 'the state-directed and state-controlled economic system pursued for the last thirty years will be gradually phased out and policy will be adopted to carry out development through a free-market-oriented economic system' (NPC 1992). Inheriting a state with a struggling economy, the new finance minister in the Nepali Congress government was committed to market reform and economic liberalisation. The liberal economic policy of the new democratic government underscored the role of private and non-government sectors and represented a paradigm shift from the excessively regulated economic regime of the past with state control in economic and social spheres (Mahat 2020, 33–34). Liberalisation made a notable mark on every single aspect of Nepal's politics and economy.

The first wave of reforms in the early 1990s focused largely on macroeconomic challenges, including stabilisation measures, trade, industry, monetary and fiscal reforms (Mahat 2020, 34). There was a massive expansion of the print and digital media, including the mushrooming of FM stations throughout Nepal. Domestic and international airlines expanded. The national air policy allowed private airlines to operate in both domestic and international sectors. Policies were made to ease foreign employment for Nepalis. Passport distribution was decentralised, so those who aspired to go abroad no longer had to come to Kathmandu, but could get their passports locally issued by the Chief District Officer.

As part of the reform programme, tariff rates were reduced, and import restriction was abolished. Export procedures were simplified. Export duties and the dual exchange rate were abolished. The banking sector was deregulated, and commercial banks were allowed to hold foreign exchange abroad. With the enactment of the Foreign Investment and Technology Transfer Act 1992, foreign investment of up to 100 per cent equity was allowed in all major sectors, including hydropower, banking, airlines and other service sectors. Reforms were also introduced in tax structure and tax administration. A value-added tax (VAT) system was introduced, and the personal income tax slabs were reduced to just two: 15 per cent and 25 per cent. Similarly, corporate tax was fixed at 25 per cent, except 30 per cent for banks and other financial institutions. The hydropower sector was opened to domestic and foreign capital. There was also a review of government-owned enterprises that were making losses and imposing a budgetary burden. By 2003, 24 enterprises were either privatised or liquidated, using various modalities depending on the nature of the concerned entity (Mahat 2020, 39). The cooperative sector and microcredit organisations were encouraged through new legislation to promote income-generating activities in rural areas (Mahat 2020, 40). Such a microfinance model shifted the onus for financial discipline and accountability onto communities, particularly women (Rankin 2001). There was a massive expansion of banking and financial institutions in the private sector, including the restructuring of the two government banks with international management teams that held up to 60 per cent of total deposits (Mahat 2020, 36).

Liberalisation of the economy meant that the health and education sectors saw a phenomenal increase in the provision of healthcare through hospitals and the training of healthcare professionals as well as rapid growth in private schools, colleges and universities. Under the rentier model, giving licenses to open health and educational institutions became a source of rent for the political class. In particular, the establishment of medical colleges and awarding licenses to train medical students with high fees has been associated with rent generation by the economic and political elite. In recent years, this pattern has come into the attention of civil society activists, under the leadership of Dr Govinda K.C., calling for the end of 'medical mafia' in Nepal. The weak regulatory mechanism has led to a massively disruptive impact from the rising costs of health and education.

The liberalisation of Nepal's economy was not accompanied by job creation. Jobs in the formal sector of the economy were limited to the civil service, NGOs and limited private-sector jobs in banks and financial institutions. The agricultural sector remained unproductive and stagnant. There was no industrialisation or any concrete policy on job creation. Despite heightened aspirations, while the economy grew in the initial years, joblessness left the youth with no work and no hope. The young people had little choice other than to out-migrate in search of work opportunities, and a few were attracted to violent politics.

Once again, while progressive constitutional changes were made and the economy was liberalised, economic freedoms did not follow. While the organisational networks of political parties opened avenues for wider participation, the old patronage system and caste system continued. Those in influential positions, in the army, judiciary and bureaucracy, and politicians continued to come from the landed class and upper-caste backgrounds. During this period, NGOs flourished. They attracted human rights activists and Left-leaning politicians, and it is often said that the Left political party, UML, received organisational and financial support from these NGOs, or at least provided employment to the family members of the party members. If there was one sector where jobs were created in visible form, it was in the NGO sector, with donors' support.

The idea of democracy and the politics of distribution, either through job creation/labour or social protection provisions did not kick off. Limited jobs were created in the service sectors in cities. With no prospect of earning income from agriculture or secure jobs in cities, people were forced to work in unskilled, poorly paid precarious jobs in the informal sectors, or were forced to out-migrate. While macroeconomic indicators seemed positive and some still regard the initial years of the 1990s as the golden decade in Nepal's development, there was a widespread perception of growing corruption and frustration among the youth and poor in particular. The Maoist movement, which started in 1996, closed any prospect of the distribution of development benefits, but provided a new vision for the radical restructuring of the Nepali state and its economy.

1996–2005: Conflict and Development

The Maoist conflict (1996–2006), which started as a rural insurgency in the hills of western Nepal and eventually spread to almost all 75 districts, presented specific challenges to the development of Nepal. Not only did it expose, at least from the Maoists' perspective, the narrative of development failure and systematic exclusion based on gender, class, caste and ethnicity, but it also became a key obstacle for the operation of development activities, especially in rural Nepal. Infrastructure projects, for example, road and hydropower projects, faced a major setback.

Development was at the core of Maoist ideology and strategy. Given the intrinsic link between the exercise of power in the Nepali state and development activities, it became a key target of Maoist insurgents. As a key tactic in undermining the state, the insurgents pursued a classical Maoist strategy of 'encircling the cities', forcing the police and civil servants to retreat to district headquarters (Gersony 2003, Ogura 2008). The Maoists worked to deny stable government access and presence throughout rural Nepal, which directly impacted the Nepali state-supported development activities. They refused to allow the implementation of hundreds of government-supported roads, hydropower and water systems, and put pressure on NGOs in their 'base areas' either by expelling foreign NGOs or forcing local groups to do their bidding (Shneiderman and Turin 2004). Banks and financial institutions were direct targets of violence and intimidation.

Not only did the Maoists threaten and attack, both politically and physically, the exclusionary development, but they also aspired to replace it with their alternative vision of development. As a rural insurgency, local development activities, including those that took place at the level of the village development committees, were particularly targeted. This manifested as padlocking the VDC office or obstructing road construction or other activities sponsored by the state. Given how important education had become, both the actual buildings and schooling, to the process of exclusionary development, schools also became a key Maoist target. School operation in many rural areas was conditional on Maoist approval. Maoists attempted to bring the teachers over to their side or, when teachers resisted, they were intimidated physically or otherwise. Health posts also became a Maoist target, but were allowed to function and were used by the Maoists. Many community health workers such as Village Health Workers and Maternal and Child Health Workers, who had to move around as a part of their work, had awkward encounters with the Maoist activists, including being forced to pay donations. Development workers and health workers in rural villages were also regularly stopped and intimidated by the Nepali state's security officials.

The Maoist leadership had understood that development was a critical instrument of rule, through which the Nepali state exercised its authority and legitimacy. They sought to undermine the state by targeting the 'developmental' architecture of the Nepali state, while replacing it with parallel state structures catering to developmental pursuits in areas they controlled. The Maoists' involvement in development activities, be it road construction, running their own schools or cooperatives or anti-discrimination campaigns, was informed by their desire to establish themselves as a parallel state.

In their areas of influence, the Maoists were ambivalent about development projects. They criticised aid-funded development activities as a form of imperialism responsible for the worsening social inequalities through elite capture and corruption. As such, the Maoists mostly saw development aid as a vehicle for maintaining the status quo and the pre-eminence of the dominating elites. However, such rhetoric of rejection was not outright. The language of rights that the NGOs used clashed with the Maoists' conception of rights. Evidence shows that the Maoists' practical strategy was to enable aid agencies to operate as long as they met their criteria for engagement, that is, if they were working 'for the people', not corrupt and not linked to outside political agendas. In some ways, the discourses of participatory development with its specific focus on inclusion and poor people were compatible with the Maoist agenda of societal transformation. However, most government- and donor-supported development programmes faced resistance from the rebels because of their lack of accountability to the people they were intended to serve (Shneiderman and Turin 2004), and because of the high salaries and 'perks' that many of the project staff enjoyed. Sara Shneiderman and Mark Turin characterise the Maoist 'attitude towards development and foreigners' in Dolakha district in the following terms:

> In VDCs where they have established *adhar ilakas*, [base area/local government] the Maoists have stated that development offices with foreign connections cannot stay. This is not because they are explicitly

> against development, but rather because they have seen how corrupt most of these organisations are. Usually only 50 per cent or less of their money actually goes towards development, the rest goes into people's pockets. The Maoists say that if they saw 100 per cent of the funds going directly to local development, they would consider letting the office stay. (Shneiderman and Turin 2004, 100)

Evidence suggests that the Maoists effectively denied stable access and operation to many development programmes throughout rural Nepal (Donini and Sharma 2008). Although the insurgents did not completely block or were not able to stop large-scale government or donor operations, they became a force to be reckoned with, preventing implementation of projects they disapproved of, placing their cadres in dominant positions on the users' committees and, in many cases, extracting funds from project staff or villagers to allow the project to continue. Nevertheless, with the exception of the Small Farmers Development Programme (SFDP) and credit cooperatives, local development activities appeared quite resilient to the conflict and continued to deliver services and small infrastructure to the communities. Maoists did use development programmes for their own ends by demanding donations or adjusting the programmes in their favour.

Overall, despite anti-imperialist slogans, the Maoists did not have a coherent policy on dealing with external aid actors and development agencies, bilateral aid bodies or even international charities. Despite adopting a neo-Marxist critique of foreign aid and development, visible in the Maoists' demands, political slogans and training of its cadres and combatants, their practical approach was more ambiguous and included a mixture of practical as well as some strategic thinking (Donini and Sharma 2008). As the movement progressed, the Maoists saw the work of aid agencies, in addition to the journalists, as actors who would be able to witness the abuses of the state against civilians and softened their stance. Not only were the development workers posted in rural areas offered a source of 'donation', but they also witnessed the human rights situation in these areas. The situation of 'forced donation' eased somewhat when the Maoists (and the government) formally approved the donor-supported Basic Operational Guidelines (BOGs)—a joint donor initiative formally launched in October 2003 to protect aid projects and personnel from overt manipulation and to ensure development and humanitarian space amid conflict (Donini and Sharma 2008).

The Maoists' '40-point demand', the public manifesto of the insurgency, was built around equality and rights (for example, to property and social inclusion), the inclusive delivery of services, (for example, education) and nationalism (for example, resisting Indian and Western expansionism). These were not particularly controversial and were also echoed in government, donor and I/NGO development priorities. However, while the goal of development, at least in terms of rhetoric, was similar across the spectrum of Nepal's political parties, the understanding of the causes of underdevelopment and the means of remedying them were wholly different. With the exception of the '40-point demand', the Maoists were generally vague and ambiguous on their vision of development. Land reform ranked high on their list of priorities, but the Maoists did not have any clear strategy for dealing with this politically difficult project, as we shall discuss later. 'Emphasis on self-reliance' was the nationalist rhetoric, and there was no concrete plan to address unemployment in the country. When it came to the broader agenda of restructuring the state, ethnic and other discrimination concerns were more thoroughly and strategically raised by the Maoists than employment or livelihoods.

The absence of elected representatives in the local bodies, since 2002, had affected the local government system, creating a political vacuum, which in many cases was filled by the Maoists during the insurgency. During the conflict, the 'development space', within which development activities could operate (Donini and Sharma 2008), was sharply reduced. The absence of functioning local political representatives meant that bureaucrats became in charge of the development activities and de facto 'representatives'. These bureaucrats lacked local legitimacy. In many cases, the VDC secretaries retreated to district headquarters, and people had to come to the district headquarters to get their work done, or they had to rely on informal relationships. By mid-2006, over two-thirds of the approximately 4,000 secretaries of VDCs—the lowest tier of government in rural areas—had been displaced to district headquarters (UN-OCHA 2006).

Locally, politicians' parties, often including the Maoists, established informal consensus-making committees, where unelected politicians from various political parties, active in the VDCs and DDCs, staked their claim to block grants and other resources that came to the local level. Such informal consensus among political leaders, replacing any institutionalised order of local government, served to legitimise the various compromises necessary for local government to function amid a lengthy political transition, and operated as a kind of abeyance technique, putting contested issues 'on hold' and allowing local government to proceed without undue disruption (Byrne and Shrestha 2014).

In this period, another key initiative was transferring the management of school facilities to local communities as part of the government's decentralisation process. This hybrid framework sought to both 'work with' and 'bypass' the government approaches, as it was the government legislation that recognised these new types of community groups and spelt out their roles and, yet, the purpose was to improve the efficiency and responsiveness of services over what the line ministries had been able to deliver. An important aim was to reduce the influence of national political parties on the selection of teachers. Over decades, during the Panchayat era, and continuing into the democratic regime, the patronage practice had created a large cohort of teachers who owed their jobs to their lobbying power and often felt little compulsion to show up in classrooms to teach. An amendment to the Education Act passed in 2001 empowered

School Management Committees (SMCs), rather than the district education office, to manage individual schools. The government has used this act as the basis for initiating the transfer of government schools, along with a significant annual grant of funds to run them and authority over the hiring and management of teachers to local communities. As resources began to flow to the schools, including various funds for infrastructural development and scholarships, with the management responsibility resting on the SMC, control has become a political struggle at the local level. Collusive practices, including mismanagement of funds, creation of ghost schools and false recordings have been reported.

During the insurgency, the combination of the Maoist threat to government workers and the inability to hold local elections rendered the local bodies even weaker by removing their democratic foundation. The local development groups, funded and supported by the state, were most vulnerable to the Maoist threat. These groups, formed by community-based organisations, were more resilient. Generally speaking, the latter appeared resilient during the conflict because of the community ownership that enabled these groups to bargain with the insurgents, often by giving them a share or using other tactics, to keep the flow of funds and services going. The groups argued that these funds/services/facilities did not belong to the central government, but to the community, which made it much harder for the rebels to co-opt or disrupt these group-based efforts.

An example of accommodation in Maoist-controlled areas is provided by the Department for International Development (DFID) supported Livelihoods and Forestry Programme (LFP) that developed ways to continue working effectively through Forestry User Groups (FUGs) in rural communities affected by the conflict. During the conflict, community forestry user groups experienced many shocks that challenged their resilience. Despite difficulties, the FUGs withstood much of the pressure and continued to operate effectively. Nightingale and Sharma (2014) found that the conflict-sensitive approach adopted by the FUGs contributed to the programme's continuity during the conflict period. Because the programme was grounded in the communities, neither the State nor the Maoists could manipulate it to their advantage.

The State's response was initially to view the Maoist insurgency as a law-and-order problem and was in denial of its inability to serve the rural population. Development activities continued, with some concerns for safety, but the space for development had already been reduced significantly.

Nonetheless, the development community based in the capital city was mostly in denial, and the conflict was seen as a minor irritant. Western donors in Nepal, until the 2000s, refused to accept the political nature of the conflict as grounded on exclusion, or recognise that aid had become intrinsically tied to the Nepali state, facilitating the capture of foreign funds by the elite (Donini and Sharma 2014). It was not until 2000 that the DFID contracted an SOAS academic to undertake a conflict assessment (Goodhand 2000), and only in the early 2000s did donors begin to see the Maoist insurgency, not as a law-and-order problem but a sociopolitical one.

It was only in 2002, six years into the insurgency, that donors began to grapple in any systematic way with the impact the conflict was having on traditional development programmes. A Risk Management Office (RMO) was jointly established by the DFID and the German technical cooperation office—Deutsche Gesellschaft für Technische Zusammenarbeit (GTZ) in 2002, to enable their development programmes to work safely and effectively without exacerbating the conflict. Law-and-order issues began to be framed as grievance-based conflicts, requiring political solutions. Major donors and development agencies working in Nepal started to consider new approaches on how to remain relevant and engaged within fragile situations during armed conflicts. Aid agencies started to include 'conflict-sensitive' programming in their aid modalities (Donini and Sharma 2014). Government presence was gradually confined to district headquarters, except in parts of the Terai and the Kathmandu valley. Despite this, donors and UN agencies cultivated the illusion that local government authorities were still in place and that it was possible to advance decentralisation, local governance and other development programmes through them (Donini and Sharma 2008).

As the insurgency became more popular in remote rural areas, it was widely reported on the front pages of the Nepali newspapers, such as the *Kantipur Daily*. Nevertheless, it took a long time for the development establishment to understand what was going on in the rural areas. Starting around 2002, the country assistance plans and strategies of the main donors started to mention the conflict and tried to find viable ways to address the underlying issues of structural violence and discrimination that were progressively being recognised and put on the development agenda (Donini and Sharma 2014).

From 2000, there was a growing interest among some European donor agencies in understanding the extent of caste and ethnic grievances through the lens of 'exclusion', particularly in relation to the rapid expansion of the Maoist insurgency in the country. By 2002–2003, some donors began to 'see' a causal link between the 'exclusion' of Dalits, women and minority ethnic groups and their participation in the Maoist insurgency. The DFID and the WB began a major research exercise titled 'Nepal Gender and Social Exclusion Assessment' (GSEA). Their report, published in 2005, helped push the issue of exclusion up the donor agenda. Since then, donors have begun to channel significant funding towards work on gender, caste and ethnicity issues through the lenses of inclusion and empowerment of these groups.

At another level, the Maoist conflict had a significant impact in escalating outmigration from rural areas to cities and towns, and from Nepal to other countries. First, the Maoist tactics forcibly displaced landed and 'enemy classes' from rural areas. Many rural landlords and powerful classes left their rural homes and properties and moved to district headquarters or the capital city of Kathmandu. This process had a huge impact on the real estate business in Kathmandu and other cities, where prices became massively inflated, while land prices in remote rural areas became depressed. While the practice was not widespread, Maoists captured and distributed land to poor peasants in some areas. Conflict and lack of any economic activity meant an increase in outmigration from Nepal, with young people seeking to leave the country at any cost. Jobs were lost in the vital tourism and hospitality sectors. The earning from remittances again fuelled the speculative real estate business and encouraged internal migration in terms of relocation of the landed class from rural areas to cities and towns. The plotting of land to build houses has been a major development in cities, as has the growth of the construction and housing industries to serve the middle classes. Thus, the Maoist insurgency coincided with a major economic change in Nepal, that is, commodification of land and labour as never before, with the deepening of the market in the citizens' everyday lives.

2006–2015: Peace Process and State-Restructuring

Following the end of the Maoist insurgency, through the UN-mediated peace process and the state restructuring, the Nepali state acquired a new identity: republic, federal and secular. This was a major departure from the centralised monarchical Hindu states of the past. Nepal's Comprehensive Peace Agreement (CPA), signed in 2006, set a roadmap for the short-term end of conflict and long-term restructuring of the Nepali state. This 'restructuring' of the state was, however, heavily tilted towards political reform, focused on demands of federalism, security sector reform and calls for equality and justice. Although the Maoist insurgency was based on socio-economic inequalities and grievances, which involved the insurgents attacking banks, land registration officers and eliminating their class enemies, such as landlords, in rural areas, these issues have been left largely ignored and unaddressed.

Of the 40-point demand of the Maoists put forward in February 1996, 13 points outlined economic justice issues. These demands included the distribution of land to the landless, guaranteed employment, minimum wage, loan relief for farmers, free health and education and the promotion of cottage industries. However, as the Maoists eventually came to the peace talks and ultimately to an agreement, the specificities of these economic agendas, as well as their prioritisation, were watered down. As the insurgency lingered on, the Maoists' call for ethnic inclusion had found a substantial uptake, especially with the unilateral demarcation of ethnic provinces, which helped the Maoists fill their rank and file with recruits from marginalised ethnic groups and get support from a variety of ethnicities. However, their agenda for economic justice had few takers; it was neither at par with the ethnic inclusion agenda in terms of galvanising the Maoist recruitment from various marginalised groups, nor did it have a fixed constituency to drive it forward, unlike the various ethnic groups who championed the inclusion agenda. While, by design or default, the Maoists had largely forsaken the agenda of economic justice, and it also failed to be articulated by the civil society groups or by public intellectuals and academics. Nepal has not yet seen any notable movement from the civil society calling for economic justice or social protection.

Civil society participation was critical to the success of the 'people's movement of 2006' (also known in Nepal as 'Janandolan II') that preceded the agreement between the Seven Party Alliance and the Maoists, and the Comprehensive Peace Agreement (CPA). This led to the mainstreaming of agendas, such as inclusion and state-restructuring within the peace process (Shah, 2008). While civil society groups, divided among themselves, applauded agendas of state-restructuring and proportional representation of marginalised groups in state organs, they too largely ignored economic justice issues.

Not surprisingly, the terms of the CPA, while it mentions issues of economic justice, the vagueness of the articles, as well as their relative obscurity compared to other provisions, has ensured that critical economic issues have neither been advocated by social and political movements nor have they been raised or addressed by the state. The CPA's Article 3, titled 'Political-Economic-Social Transformation and Conflict Management', called for the end of all forms of feudalism, implementation of scientific land-reform programmes, protection of national industries and resources and protection for economically backward sections. However, these commitments lacked specific detail, and unlike the different commissions formed to sketch the details of political issues like federalism or transitional justice, no concrete mechanisms were instituted for these issues and, inevitably, nothing has been implemented. The result of this neglect of the economic justice agenda means that, despite a history of systematic marginalisation of the peasantry, through unequal land distribution, exploitation through free labour and extraction of rent, the broader discussion on inclusion in the peace process omitted questions about the Nepali peasants and the poor. Furthermore, Article 7.5.5. of the CPA stated, 'Both sides agree that the private property of any individual would not be seized or usurped, except permitted by the laws.' This formally paved the way to the release of land captured by the former rebels to the registered owners of the land.

The only specific point under Article 3.3 of the CPA was to limit the authority of the king, including nationalising the properties received by the king in his capacity as monarch. It stated:

> 3.3. To not allow any authority regarding affairs of governance of the country to remain with the King. To bring the properties of late King Birendra, late queen Aishwarya and their family under Government of Nepal and to make use of the property in the interest of the state by forming a trust. To nationalise all the properties (like palaces situated in different places, forest and parks, heritages with historical

> and archaeological importance) received by King Gyanendra in his capacity as the King. To decide the issue of whether or not to retain the monarchy by simple majority in the first meeting of constituent assembly. (Article 3.3)

While symbolically very important, the above provision on its own did not address the historical source of 'state landlordism' (Regmi 1977). Other articles of the CPA that mentioned economic justice were very broad and lacked specific content. Thus, there has not been any progress on a 'programme for the economic or social transformation to end all forms of feudalism' (Article 3.6). The promise of 'scientific land reforms program by ending feudal land ownership' (Article 3.7) and 'the policy of providing land and other economic protection to socially and economically backward classes including land less squatters, bonded laborers and pastoral farmers' (Article 3.10) have not been followed up. The aspiration 'to follow a policy of protecting and promoting national industries and resources' (Article 3.8) has not seen any concrete plan in the last decade and a half. The agreement 'to adopt policy of establishing the rights of all citizens to education, health, housing, employment and food security' (Article 3.9) has not been followed by any specific measures to address access to basic services. Instead, out-of-pocket health expenditure has increased. As hundreds and thousands of Nepalis rush to migrate to different migrant labour destinations, the agreement on job creation, as articulated in Article 3.13—'to follow a policy of massive increase in employment and income generation opportunities by increasing investment in industries, trade and export promotion, etc. while ensuring the professional rights of the laborers'—has remained a distant dream.

Not only did the CPA overlook economic justice, but the protracted political transition and the continually changing political landscape have also inhibited Nepal's overall macro-economic prospects. In this period, economic growth has remained sluggish. While the end of the conflict was said to have increased economic confidence and improved the investment climate, job creation has been slow, and there have been no major initiatives for social protection. Due to the protracted nature of the political transition and the low-intensity conflict followed by the devastating earthquake, there was an economic stagnation in 2016. Growth in tourism and remittances, as well as relative political stability, together with an uninterrupted power supply, has meant that economic growth has picked up thereafter with 8 per cent growth in 2017, over 6 per cent in 2018 and 7 per cent in 2019 (Blumer et al. 2020).

Limited jobs were created in Nepal's booming construction sector, transportation and commercial sectors. According to the World Bank's estimates, 4 million jobs were created between 2008 and 2018 in Nepal, with the share of wage work increased from 17 per cent to 24 per cent of total employment (Blumer et al. 2020). Many jobs were also created during the post-earthquake reconstruction. However, there have not been enough jobs to absorb all jobseekers, leading many of them to continue to seek employment abroad. According to a World Bank report, by 2018, there were 3.8 million wage jobs in Nepal, and another 2.8 million Nepalese were employed in wage jobs in other countries (Blumer et al. 2020). Lack of quality job creation and poor-quality jobs has meant that young people are desperate to out-migrate often under precarious conditions. As in the previous decades, the state allowed many Nepali youth to leave Nepal in search of labouring opportunities in key destinations such as the Gulf countries, Israel, Malaysia and South Korea, among others. Most international migrants are male, two-thirds are under the age of 35 and 85 per cent have not completed secondary education (Blumer et al. 2020).

While the sluggish economic growth and lack of jobs have created economic precarity, there has not been any notable movement from below demanding economic justice. The state has not come forward with social protection or welfare provisions to give people a cushion. While the period between 2006 and 2015 saw impressive identity-based social and political movements demanding greater rights for different ethnic, regional and linguistic groups, there has been no notable social movement demanding economic justice or putting pressure on the state to implement the commitments mentioned in CPA on issues of economic justice. The civil society and the public debate have completely ignored these commitments on economic justice. The absence of social movements or civil society mobilisations based on questions of economic justice has meant that not only have historical economic inequalities remained unaddressed, but also that there is no pressure on the Nepali state to offer programmes of social protection for those who have found themselves subject to destructive market forces, including the commodification of land and labour.

In the absence of elected local representatives, the modus operandi of post-2006 politics continued to be based on the politics of consensus in the form of an all-party mechanism. The all-party mechanism, which had the discursive element of participation and consensus, replaced decision-making on development and resource allocation at local and national levels. In theory, the all-party mechanism promoted informal deliberative practices at the local level. This system continued till 2017, when the local elections were finally held.

As discussed earlier, the all-party mechanism has its roots in 2002, when the term of locally elected officials came to an end, and the Nepali state retreated from rural areas. This mode of operation was institutionalised in 2009 when the cabinet gave political parties a consultative status. This idea closely resonated with the inclusion and participation championed by Nepal's development partners. Although the mechanism was formally abolished in 2012 amid allegations of corruption following the investigation by Nepal's Commission for Investigation of Abuse of Authority, the practice has continued. Media reports have covered stories of collusive tendencies in local politics, allocation of contracts and siphoning of resources without any accountability. The Asia Foundation 2012 report looked at this political practice in local governance and made the following analysis.

> Under the APMs, no party is uniquely positioned to monopolize public funds and resources for patronage purposes. Each is keen to increase its share of the treasury, and there is no agreed upon formula to allocate 'patronage rights' among political actors. As a result, two types of ad hoc arrangements have emerged: (1) in almost all APMs, a pecking order has been negotiated based on the results of the national election of 2008, with some reference to the local performance of the parties, and (2) with no opposition bench left, the parties have found it more profitable to collude with strategic partners in the pecking order to increase their share of the public resources. (The Asia Foundation 2012)

As widely reported in Nepali media, it has become very common to find politicians engaging in the construction business and often awarding contracts to themselves or their family members. Over time, the distribution of development goods has not translated into citizenship, but more into distributional coalitions who 'eat' resources.

As the members involved in party mechanisms are not elected by or accountable to the people, concerns have been raised on the mismanagement and siphoning of funds through consensus politics and continuation of patronage politics.

With donor support, attempts have been made to make local political mechanisms accountable through citizens' forums. The forums were expected to represent local people's voices by discussing, prioritising and overseeing development efforts at the local level. Under the Local Government and Community Development Program (LGCPD), a donor-funded programme, social mobilisers were appointed and deployed. However, social mobilisers have very little control over political dynamics at the local level.

Distributional coalitions at local and national levels continued as in previous years. Political representatives were lobbying for an increased share of the budget under their direct disbursement, calling for further strengthening of their patronage networks. In 2015, the amount allocated to the Member of Parliament Fund increased from 1 million to 11.5 million, including 1.5 million for an MP from the Proportional Representation (PR) system. This amount was increased to 15 million for directly elected MPs and 2 million for those elected through the PR system in 2016. In 2017, it increased to 30 million for the former and 5 million for the latter. In 2019, the scheme's name was changed to Constituency Development Fund, and 40 million was allocated to each constituency, which was increased to 60 million in 2020. The scale on which money is spent through MPs has led to widespread criticism of this programme for fuelling corruption.

During this period, one significant change has been the reservation for excluded groups in all state institutions, including the civil service and elections to all three tiers of government—federal, provincial and municipal—to engender gender and caste equality. By any standard, these changes are radical. The key question is whether these new equations of political power will translate to economic power.

The 2015 Earthquake, Humanitarian Assistance and the Emergence of a 'New' Nepali Nationalism

In 2015, a severe earthquake of 7.8 magnitude hit Nepal, creating an unprecedented national calamity. Its ramifications, however, were beyond physical destruction (Hutt et al. 2021). The plans for reconstruction and recovery from the earthquake had political and economic ramifications, seeking to alter patterns of distribution of rent and resources, often using the rhetoric of reconstruction and development. In the economic realm, the distribution of reconstruction aid as well as the channelling of foreign aid to rebuilding efforts, while partially supporting victims, was mired in allegations of corruption, the politicisation of appointments in institutions formed for recovery as well as centralisation of decision-making (Pokharel et al. 2018). Politically, the earthquake provided a pretext to claw back on inclusion-related guarantees committed to by the Interim Constitution, through mechanisms like federalism, electoral laws and quotas—all of which would decentralise power and competition for rents (Roy and Khan 2017). Citing the earthquake and the necessity to prioritise reconstruction efforts, the Constitution writing process was fast-tracked and adopted in 2015. This Constitution of 2015, which had been in the making since 2008, relied on a 16-point agreement between four main political parties to decide on all substantive aspects of the Constitution, rather than the deliberations at the Constitution Assembly, reneging on multiple inclusion-related guarantees.

To start with, despite scientists having long predicted an earthquake in the region, the Nepali government appeared totally unprepared to address the scale of devastation. The UN Office for the Coordination of Humanitarian Affairs (OCHA) estimated that approximately 2.8 million people, around 10 per cent of Nepal's population, required humanitarian assistance. As of 30 June 2015, there were 8,844 causalities and over 22,300 injuries. A total of 446 public health facilities and 16 private health facilities were completely destroyed, and a total of 765 health facility structures were partially damaged. As a result, health facilities' ability to respond to healthcare needs had been affected, and service delivery was disorganised. School buildings were damaged, leaving pupils out of school, which is likely to impact enrolment, attendance and internal efficiency, leading to an increase in the number of children not attending school. Half a million houses were destroyed and a quarter million houses were partially damaged. Preliminary assessments suggested that the earthquake was 'classed', meaning that it disproportionately affected the poorer and those in rural locations. Most mud-built houses collapsed. Post-Disaster Needs Assessment showed that the recovery costs amounted to one-third of the economy. The WB estimated that about 3 per cent more Nepali people had been pushed into poverty.

The scale of the devastation would be a challenge for any government, but the ingrained features of Nepal's political economy worsened prospects of an effective response. Nepal's ability to respond quickly and effectively was not only hampered by geographical remoteness, poor infrastructure and lack of facilities (such as limited road access, limited access to equipment and only one airport), but also by institutional gaps, such as the lack of effective leadership, absence of local government, lack of coordination and weak governance (Sharma et al. 2018).

As indicated earlier, the absence of elected representatives in the local bodies, which had been run by government staff and the all-party mechanism, for the last 13 years, meant that there was no reliable system ready to deliver aid to districts and villages. The institutional vacuum, left by over 16 years of absence of the local government, meant that not only did people not have a legitimate political institution to hear and echo their voice as a local government should, but, in some cases, unaffected local elites were included in the lists of victims receiving financial support (Pokharel et al. 2018).

With no institutional body to manage the response, the first to respond were the locals followed by the army, armed police and Nepal Police mobilised by the government for initial rescue and relief work. Nepali diaspora groups were quick to engage through their familial and kinship networks. The Indian National Disaster Response Force (NDRF), Indian Air Force and Indian Army Medical Corps were the first foreign response teams to land in Kathmandu within hours of the disaster to help launch relief operations, followed by teams from China. Overall, the Nepali State mobilised 22,500 civil servants, 65,059 staff of the Nepal Army, 41,776 staff of the Nepal Police and 24,775 staff of the Armed Police Force. In addition, 4,000 government and private health workers were deployed to aid rescue and relief efforts.

Added to the domestic equation were the flow and impact of the foreign aid that poured into the reconstruction process. Once local and international journalists and locals began to capture and share the images and descriptions of suffering, they began to circulate quickly through traditional as well as social media, encouraging aid from within the country, from neighbouring India, China,

Bhutan and Pakistan, as well as from other countries. Patterns of aid also conformed to the long-standing geopolitical priorities that characterised Nepal's history of foreign assistance. Located between India and China, a geographical situation that has always shaped foreign aid and international engagement in Nepal continued to inform the humanitarian assistance. The initial occupation of Nepal's only airport by the Indian Air Force, built in the early 1950s with Indian assistance for strategic reasons, meant that there was very little space available for other countries to fly in with their relief aid. The airport was later opened after the Chinese government and others complained about congestion at the airport. As India and China intensified their supply of military aircraft and helicopters for relief, the US mobilised Osprey aircraft, which can land and take off vertically, that landed in Kathmandu almost after a week, on 3 May 2015. On the other hand, the Government of Nepal asked the UK not to send their heavy-lift Chinook twin-rotor helicopters to the country. While the official reason given by the government was the fear of 'downwash' from the larger rotorcraft, speculation was rife in the media that it was possibly due to a trial initiated by the UK government against a Nepal Army colonel under universal jurisdiction, and, possibly, partly due to leverage on the part of China and India to avoid Western presence in Nepal. *The Times*, London, quoted an anonymous source, who said: 'The Chinese aren't that keen on lots of foreign military around in that area. The Indians don't like foreign military flying around and the Nepalese are being difficult because they can't have any control over them.'[2] Likewise, the Taiwanese government was asked not to participate, possibly due to pressure from China.

Two months after the first earthquake, on 25 June 2015, the Government of Nepal organised a donor conference in Kathmandu. The conference ended with a pledge of 4.4 billion USD for Nepal's

2 *The Times*, London, 12 May 2015. Available at: https://www.thetimes.co.uk/article/nepal-blocks-british-chinooks-from-earthquake-relief-mission-mgkd90dhtx2 (Accessed on 10 February 2021).

reconstruction by donors, half in grants and about half in loans. More globally, the UN Flash Appeal for support launched on 29 April 2015 requested a total of 422 million USD to meet critical humanitarian needs. As of 7 July 2015, a total of 195.4 million USD, including 15 million USD from Central Emergency Relief Fund, had been contributed. As international relief aid agencies made it to earthquake-affected areas, including INGOs and NGOs that had a long history of working on development, conflict and peace-related activities before, during and after the Maoist insurgency, joined the relief work. As of 23 June 2015, the UN OCHA reported that 387 agencies were working in the earthquake-affected areas.

Outsourcing of humanitarian assistance through a chain of different international, national and local actors was a key feature. Humanitarian agencies delivered relief aid through existing organisations, mainly through the UN system, major humanitarian NGOs such as Save the Children, Oxfam, World Vision and the Red Cross/RC movement. One estimate suggested that local organisations, based in Nepal, applied for less than 1 per cent of the budget and most of the aid went through major transnational players/agencies. Tabulation by journalist Emily Troutman indicates that only $3.5 million or 0.8 per cent of the total $422 million in proposed projects will actually go to the Nepalese NGOs. Ultimately, the relief aid was distributed through local organisations through subcontractual agreements that raised several questions on the transaction cost and accountability of relief work.

There was widespread criticism of the relief agencies that were operating with little or no coordination and accountability. Different organisations were often found to be taking credit for the same work. Relief agencies misreported their overhead costs by excluding the expenses incurred by their many subcontractors. A survey by the Disaster Accountability Project, a nonprofit that promotes transparency and oversight in disaster management systems, revealed that scores of agencies, collecting money for relief in Nepal, diverted the funds to other projects, the details of which were not specified. Often humanitarian agencies had their own campaigns through media and social media, with digitalised infographics showing the number of goods distributed, the number of people reached and other details. However, there was very little clarity on how such numbers had been calculated.

As relief goods and humanitarian aid began to pour into the country, the government was under pressure to coordinate aid. The Nepali state was severely criticised for red tape and bureaucracy that extended from airport clearance to relief coordination at the district level. *The Guardian* reported that customs delays were hampering relief efforts in Nepal and quoted the UN Resident Coordinator as saying, 'They (government) should not be using peacetime customs methodology…'[3] The government was critical of international relief aid on many grounds. In one instance, the Finance Minister was quoted as saying, 'We have received things like tuna fish and mayonnaise. What good are those things for us? We need grains, salt and sugar.'

Due to a lack of strong political leadership and partly overwhelmed by the spontaneous response from locals, mostly youth, and international relief aid and its visibility in the media, there was widespread criticism of the Nepali State. On the one hand, the State was criticised for its inability to take the lead in relief aid and reach out to those affected by the earthquake in remote areas, while, on the other hand, paradoxically, it was criticised for making an attempt to control relief aid in the form of regulation and requests for documentation. In sum, the absence of coordination and geopolitical divides further compounded the ineffective response by the government. Such ineptitude has been admitted by the government, as the Chief Secretary wrote, 'I admit that we didn't have capability and preparedness to handle a disaster of such magnitude. Even if we did, we would not be able to maintain that scale of resources, all the

3 *The Guardian*, London, 2 May 2015. Available at: https://www.theguardian.com/world/2015/may/02/nepal-customs-holding-up-relief-jamie-mcgoldrick-united-nations (Accessed on 10 February 2021).

time, in anticipation of such disaster.'[4] A social audit carried out by a Kathmandu-based academic NGO, Martin Chautari, found that the Nepali state had, for years, been collecting documents that could have helped organise the relief work, but failed to use them.[5]

The government did eventually form the National Reconstruction Authority with the rationale that employing regular government institutions could cause delays.[6] However, the Nepal Reconstruction Authority (NRA) swiftly fell into an abyss of criticism of politicisation, clientelism and corruption—unable to escape these features that have long characterised Nepali political economy. Institutions, and the rents that flow from them have always been politicised in Nepal, but the scale of the recovery operation, supported both domestically and with swathes of foreign aid, meant that the NRA and post-quake recovery projects in general fell prey to clientelism. For example, appointments to the NRA became disputed, with different parties wanting to appoint people sympathetic to their party. Political differences about the organisation's leadership meant that it took almost nine months to appoint someone to lead the NRA, which delayed its operations and the resulting delivery of services (Pokharel et al. 2018). Additionally, the leadership of the NRA changed with every change in the government. 'Even in the desperate days of reconstruction, NRA welcomed its new CEO2 on October 23, 2017, after the resignation of earlier CEO3 who was himself appointed in January 2017 a second time. This makes the present CEO the fourth in the row of fewer than 3 years after the earthquake' (Sharma et al. 2018, 764–765).

Added to the politicisation were widespread complaints about the modalities of NRA's operations. Multiple forms of assistance were deployed from the initial cash grant, winter relief and the Nepal Rural

4 http://archive.myrepublica.com/2015-16/opinion/story/20641/from-the-horse-s-mouth.html (accessed on 10 February 2021).

5 https://kathmandupost.com/opinion/2015/06/09/remembering-to-forget (accessed on 10 February 2021).

6 https://kathmandupost.com/national/2019/11/13/national-reconstruction-authority-spent-just-65-per cent-of-its-budget-last-fiscal-year (accessed on 10 February 2021).

Housing Reconstruction Programme to rebuild damaged homes, which was disbursed in three tranches. Changes in governments also brought changes in the terms of these grants. For instance, the prime ministership of Pushpa Kamal Dahal, between August 2016 and May 2017, brought a raft of changes to the grant modalities. An additional रु100,000 was added to the housing reconstruction grant, taking the total available for fully damaged houses to रु300,000. Many households that did not have documentation started applying for official documents and opening bank accounts. The flow of money for reconstruction, in addition to remittances, has intensified financialisation in rural Nepal (Le Billon et al. 2000).

Beyond the immediate impact on the economy, and lives and livelihoods, the earthquake had a seismic impact on Nepal's long political transition. Taking the earthquake as a pretext, the government decided to 'fast-track the constitution-writing process', pleading the need to focus on rebuilding efforts. As mentioned before, an agreement between the leaders of four major political parties had decided on all the contentious issues of the Constitution, which had yet to be finalised in the Constituent Assembly. The 16-point agreement between these four parties included the number of provinces, procedures for the naming of provinces, nature of the parliament, electoral system, forms of government and the judicial system. In making these commitments, these agreements not only undercut the deliberations going on in the Constituent Assembly, but also saw major reversals on multiple inclusion-related commitments. For instance, provincial boundaries were delineated in ways which prioritised the capacity of the provinces for development, rather than identity. Throughout the history of Nepal's constitution-writing process, there have been political divisions about whether the boundaries for federal provinces should prioritise issues of identity (ethnicity, community, language, culture, regional and historical continuity) or capacity (availability of natural resources, the status of development infrastructure and administrative convenience). Further, quota provisions in the Constitution had included policies, such as 33 per cent female representation in all organs of the state as well as the allocation of 45 per cent of civil service seats for marginalised groups. However, the 2015 Constitution further weakened this agreement, by adding the already over-represented category of 'Khas Arya' as one of the 'communities' entitled to reservation. The mixed electoral system of 40 per cent representation through 'First-Past-The-Post (FPTP)', and 56 per cent through Proportional Representation, which had successfully resulted in political parties allocating seats to members of marginalised groups was reversed to 40 per cent representation from PR and 60 per cent through FPTP. Equal citizenship rights to women were also denied, and foreigners married to Nepali women did not qualify for Nepali citizenship. Their children were only eligible for naturalised citizenship (Rai 2018).

Despite these problems, strong party whips and a record number of articles being passed in under 11 hours led to the Constitution being promulgated with 507 of the 598 members of the Assembly voting for the new Constitution in September 2015.

However, the new Constitution failed to appease various marginalised groups, who resorted to protests along the southern border. The protests by Madhesi parties called for the Constitution to honour past agreements as well as reflect the spirit of the Madhesi movement and demanded proportional and inclusive representation, delineation of constituencies based on population, changes to the federal demarcation of boundaries and citizenship. A part of the protest was a blockade of the Indo–Nepal border, which, owing to Nepal's landlocked geography, choked off supplies to the rest of the country. While the Madhesi agitation was seen by many as a legitimate struggle for equal presentation and representation, the timing of the blockades impeded the recovery from the disaster of the earthquake. With supply routes blocked, the human rights aspect of the Madhesi protests was seen to have interfered with post-earthquake humanitarian relief.

The regional and international dimension to the Constitution's promulgation added a further layer of complexity, triggering an avalanche of nationalistic sentiments. On the grounds that the Constitution had not addressed the concerns of the Madhesis, which the Nepali political leaders were said to have guaranteed India, and supposed concerns about the spill-over of the instability to Indian territory, India 'only noted' the promulgation of the Constitution (Muni 2015). While China 'noted with pleasure' the promulgation, others, like the US, and blocs like the EU, welcomed it, albeit identifying a few deficiencies. The Indian apprehension with the Constitution and its informal support to the blockade sparked an unprecedented nationalistic sentiment in Nepal, attributing the demands of the Madhesi groups to Indian interests. The growing nationalism, often taking the form of anti-India sentiment, also led to Nepal looking to strengthen its relationship with China—a circular history echoing the geopolitics of the 1960s.

The nationalistic backlash, however, was not limited to India. Western donors also drew fire from the government, on the grounds of the Western donors and multilateral institutions bolstering the drive to promote the inclusion of marginalised groups, as well as pointing out the inclusion-related regressions in the new Constitution. The government-mobilised sovereignty-related discourses, which added to the growing anti-India and anti-West sentiments associated with Nepal's political transition, have led to a rise in Right-wing nationalism in Nepal. The election of transitional political parties, like the NC and UML, and the loss of the Maoist and Madhesi parties in the second Constituent Assembly election, had already heralded an elite backlash against the sea changes brought forth by the Interim Constitution. However, the Constitution's promulgation against the backdrop of the earthquake cemented a regressive and nationalistic course of politics.

Multiple occurrences demonstrated an increased hostility towards the international community. A British ambassador's article, in a Nepali newspaper, arguing for the right to convert to a different religion, led people to view secularism as a Western agenda, the aim of which was the proselytisation of Hindus.[7] Similarly, the EU Election Observation Mission's recommendations, on Nepal's reservation policy, incurred the wrath of political leaders, including the Prime Minister, who labelled it as an infringement of the country's sovereignty and territorial integrity.[8] In yet another instance, a report titled 'Forging Equal Citizenship in a Multicultural Nepal', funded by the DFID and the Asian Development Bank, was shelved, after alleged pressure from the Caste Hill Hindu Elite (Drucza 2017). By the same token, the Nepali government is alleged to have diluted the inclusion-related content of the UN Development Assistance Framework (UNDAF), which guides the work of the UN in Nepal (Drucza 2017).

Overall, the 2015 earthquake was a major event in Nepal's political history. While it led to the conclusion of Nepal's constitutional settlement, albeit through a majoritarian push, its legacy has been exclusionary, leading to conflict in Nepal's Terai and a border blockade that resulted in high humanitarian costs. The nationalistic and sovereignty-led sentiments, expressed in terms of anti-India and anti-West sentiments, have grown significantly, leading to a slow consolidation of Right-wing Nepali hill nationalism. Nepal's constitutional settlement of 2015, following the earthquake, has made politics more regressive and nationalistic. Against the background of the earthquake, there has been an elite backlash against some of the progressive agendas on inclusion and the emergence of sovereignty-led discourses against donors.

While there have been significant amendments to the Constitution, notably on the number of provinces as well as the delineation of political constituencies based on population, the prospects of the new Nepal promised by the peace process remains a work in progress. Further,

7 https://kathmandupost.com/miscellaneous/2014/12/16/diplomat-summoned-over-envoys-conversion-note (accessed on 10 February 2021).

8 https://kathmandupost.com/national/2018/03/26/lawmakers-condemns-eus-election-observation-report (Accessed on 10 February 2021).

in the elections conducted as per the new Constitution, in all three levels of the government—local, provincial and national—narratives of development and nationalism have been at the core of political mobilisations. The 'Left Alliance', an alliance of the UML and the Maoists, which came to power in 2017, campaigned on the pledge of 'stability for prosperity'. The election, thus, marked a significant departure from the post-conflict political interregnum in Nepal, where demands for social justice and inclusion were replaced by slogans of prosperity and economic development. This idea of prosperity resonated with similar political slogans of authoritarian rulers in China and India.

The transition to reinstated local bodies and newly instituted provincial bodies has meant that a larger share of public funds is now controlled at the local level, decentralising rent patterns. The seven provinces have started drawing up their own five-year plans, setting targets for high economic growth and living standards, as well as lobbying for financial packages for their developmental planning to the Centre. Moreover, with local-level elections in 2017/2018, the local bodies are now filling the vacuum created when their tenure expired in 2002. The transition to a three-tiered system, which reflects the principles of good governance, local participation and inclusion at its core, has been engendered by informal sharing of rents, both formally and informally, often at the cost of development and prosperity. For instance, at the national level, the Left Alliance's electoral victory, which promised some form of constitutional stability, has been mired in tussles between sharing of rents, resources and institutions between the Maoists and the UML. With the transition to the federal arrangement, and the expanded bureaucratic and institutional systems, appointments to posts within these structures have been particular bargaining points. The Maoists have threatened to dissolve the Left Alliance over issues such as sharing prime ministerial terms between the two party leaders, promoting and transferring security officials and bureaucrats and appointment of cabinet ministers. At the federal level, a power-sharing model between the three tiers of government has been of particular contention. A power tussle has been reported between the provincial and federal authorities on administrative powers, resources and clarity over constitutional provisions and rights. At the local level, collusion between different political parties on development-funding has continued unabated, and, ironically, has become more sophisticated and institutionalised.

Thus, while stability on formal and informal power-sharing of rents and resources between different political parties at all levels has been achieved, it has meant a compromise on developmental indicators and growth. Indeed, it has heralded a perverse form of democracy, which functions only due to a high degree of participation in collusion in the distribution of rents at all levels. This has led to questions about the costs of federalism for a country like Nepal. While federalism was proposed as a panacea for inclusive growth in the peace process, the staggering costs have fomented growing disenchantment and an elite backlash.

Conclusion

Development in Nepal, post 1950, has been profoundly shaped by its history of unequal distribution of land, caste and patronage system. Radical political changes, installation of democratic institutions and new sources of power and rent have altered the political economy of development. The significance of rural landholding, a key source of power and inequality, has been in decline. Traditionally, the rent has been primarily extracted from land-based sources, such as agriculture, taxation or labour. New sources of power and capital accumulation, through the rent generated from labour migrant remittances and the labour migration industry, the commodification of labour, land, education and health, amid the declining significance of agriculture and rural landholding, have reconfigured the political economy. Power does not just emanate from landholding and caste-based configurations, but also through access to education, new social, political and economic networks and new rent sources. New sources of rent for the economic and political elite emanate from Nepal's migration industry, including remittance transfer, the commodification of education and health and the growing real estate and construction businesses.

Post 1950, political regimes and their networks have used development and the political and economic power associated with it to consolidate their hold on power or used it to further their patronage networks. This continued within the framework of *bikas* within the Panchayat system, which used the power and money associated with it to consolidate the regime, and, so, the process of democratisation did not result in a transformation in patronage networks. Instead, the old patronage networks continued to work under the guises of political parties, user groups, civil society, people's participation and local democracy. In addition to the old caste-based political, military and bureaucratic establishment that continued to wield power in the new political system, despite the new rhetoric, newly elected representatives, as well as local user groups and committees, have also indulged in clientelist modes of operation.

Nonetheless, the discourses of inclusion have meant that emergent political networks have not always been solely controlled by historically dominant upper-caste groups, but also by emergent horizontal networks. The politics of the distribution of development has been realised in practice by distributional coalitions. Understanding these emergent forms of political and economic networks would require an analysis that does not limit itself to an evaluation of development.

References

Adhikari, K.R. 1996. 'Naming Ceremonies As Rituals of Development'. *Studies in Nepali History and Society*, 1(2): 345–364.

Adhikari, M. 2014. 'Politics and Perceptions of Indian Aid to Nepal'. *Strategic Analysis*, 38(3): 325–340.

Blaikie, P., J. Cameron, and D. Seddon. 1980. *Nepal in Crisis: Growth and Stagnation at the Periphery*. Delhi: Oxford University Press.

Bulmer, R.E., A. Shrestha, and M. Marshalian. 2020. *Jobs Diagnostic Nepal*. Washington: World Bank.

Byrne, S. and G. Shrestha. 2014. 'A Compromising Consensus? Legitimising Local Government in Post-conflict Nepal'. *International Development Planning Review*, 36(4): 434–453.

Dixit, K.M. 1997. 'Foreign Aid in Nepal: No Bang for the Buck'. *Studies in Nepali History and Society*, 2(1):173–186.

Donini, A. and J.R. Sharma. 2008. *Humanitarian Agenda 2015: Nepal Case Study*. Medford, Massachusetts: Feinstein International Center, Tufts University.

Donini, A. and J.R. Sharma. 2014. 'Aid and Violence: Development, Insurgency and Social Transformation in Nepal'. In *Civil War in South Asia: Sovereignty and citizenship*, edited by A. Sundar and N. Sundar, 117–141. Delhi: SAGE Publications.

Drucza, K. 2017. 'Social Inclusion in the Post-Conflict State of Nepal: Donor Practice and the Political Settlement'. *Global Social Policy*, 17(1): 62–88.

Fujikura, T. 2013. *Discourses of Awareness: Development, Social Movements and the Practices of Freedom in Nepal*. Kathmandu: Martin Chautari.

Gersony, R. 2003. *Sowing the Wind...: History and Dynamics of the Maoist Revolt in Nepal's Rapti Hills*. Portland, Oregon: Mercy Corps International.

Goodhand, J. 2000. *Strategic Conflict Assessment, Nepal*. INTRAC Report Prepared for CHAD/DFID. Kathmandu: DFID.

Gyawali, B. 2017. 'Nepal's Pre-bikas Encounters with the West: Sabhyata and Unnati As Precursors to Development'. *Studies in Nepali History and Society*, 22(2): 227–260.

Gyawali, B. 2018. *Ambiguous Bikās: History of the Concept of Development in Nepal 1900–2006*, PhD Dissertation. Finland: Department of Political and Economic Studies University of Helsinki.

Gyawali, D.M., Thompson and M. Verweij, eds. 2017. *Aid, Technology and Development: The Lessons from Nepal*. London: Routledge and Earthscan.

Harper, I. 2014. *Development and Public Health in the Himalaya: Reflections on Healing in Contemporary Nepal*. London: Routledge.

Hutt, M., M. Liechty, and S. Lotter. 2021 (Forthcoming). *Epicentre to Aftermath: Rebuilding and Remembering in the Wake of Nepal's Earthquakes*. New Delhi: Cambridge University Press.

Inden, R. 1990. *Imagining India*. Oxford: Blackwell.

Ismail, F. 2017. 'Polar opposites? NGOs, Left Parties and the Fight for Social Change in Nepal'. *Critical Sociology*, 44(4–5): 629–643.

Justice, J. 1986. *Policies, Plans and People: Foreign Aid and Health Development*. Berkeley: University of California Press.

Khadka, N. 1991. 'Nepal's Stagnant Economy: The Panchayat Legacy'. *Asian Survey*, 31(8): 694–11.

Khadka, N. 1997. *Foreign Aid and Foreign Policy: Major Powers and Nepal*. New Delhi: Vikas Publishing.

Le Billon, M.S. Phillippe, J. Baniya, B. Limbu, D. Paudel, K. Rankin, N. Rawal, and S. Schneiderman. 2020. 'Disaster Financialization: Earthquakes, Cashflows, and Shifting Household Economies'. *Development and Change*, 51(4): 939–969.

Levine, NE. 1987. 'Caste, State and Ethnic Boundaries in Nepal'. *Journal of Asian Studies*, 46 (1): 71–88.

Lewis, D. and D. Mosse, eds. 2006. *Development Brokers and Translators: The Ethnography of Aid Agencies*. Bloomfield, CT: Kumarian Press.

Liechty, M. 2017. *Far Out: Countercultural Seekers and the Tourist Encounter in Nepal*. Chicago and London: University of Chicago Press.

Mahat, R.S. 2020. *Trials, Tremors and Hope: The Political Economy of Contemporary Nepal*. New Delhi: Adroit Publishers.

Metz, J.J. 1995. 'Development in Nepal: Investment in the Status Quo'. *Geo Journal*, 35(2): 175–184.

Mihaly, E.B. 1965. *Foreign Aid and Politics in Nepal: A Case Study*. London and New York: Oxford University Press.

Mishra, C. 1987. 'Development and Underdevelopment. A Preliminary Sociological Perspective'. *Occasional Papers in Sociology and Anthropology*, 1: 105–135. Available at http://himalaya.socanth. cam.ac.uk/collections/journals/opsa/pdf/OPSA_01_09.pdf (Accessed on 20 September 2020).

Mosse, D. 2005. *Cultivating Development: An Ethnography of Aid Policy and Practice*. London: Pluto Press.

Muni, SD. 2015. 'Nepal's New Constitution: Towards Progress or Chaos?'. *Economic and Political Weekly*, L (40): 15–19.

Nickson, A. 1992. 'Foreign Aid and Foreign Policy: The Case of British Aid to Nepal'. *Papers in the Administration of Development* 48. Development Administration Group, University of Birmingham.

Nightingale, A. and J. R. Sharma. 2014. 'Community Forestry User-Groups and Conflict: Experiences of a Donor Supported Community Forestry Programme in Nepal'. *Disasters* 38(4): 515–539.

Ogura, K. 2008. 'Maoist People's Governments, 2001–05: The Power in Wartime'. In *Local Democracy in South Asia: Microprocesses of Democratization in Nepal and Its Neighbours*, edited by D.N. Geller and K. Hachethu, 175–231. Delhi: Sage.

Pandey, D.R. 1999. *Nepal's Failed Development.* Kathmandu: Nepal South Asia Centre.

Pant, Y.P. 1956. 'Nepal Has a Five-Year Plan'. *The Economic Weekly*, 8:113–117.

Pfaff-Czarnecka, J. 2008. 'Distributional Coalitions in Nepal: An Essay on Democratization, Capture, and (Lack of) Confidence'. In *Local Democracy in South Asia: Microprocesses of Democratization in Nepal and its Neighbours*, edited by D.N. Gellner and K. Hachhethu, 71–104. New Delhi: Sage.

Pigg, S.L. 1992. 'Inventing Social Categories through Place—Social Representations and Development in Nepal'. *Comparative Studies in Society and History*, 34: 491–513.

Pigg, S.L. 1993. 'Unintended Consequences: The Ideological Impact of Development in Nepal'. *South Asia Bulletin*, 13(1 and 2): 45–58.

Pokharel, T., M.D. Manandhar, A. Dahal, B. Chalise, R. Bhandari and T.P. Kharel. 2018. *Political Analysis of Post-Earthquake Reconstruction in Nepal: An Assessment of Emerging Role of Local Governments*. Kathmandu: Nepal Administrative Staff College and The Asia Foundation.

Rankin, K.N. 2001. 'Governing Development: Neoliberalism, Microcredit, and Rational Economic Woman'. *Economy and Society*, 30 (1): 18–37.

Rankin, K. 2004. *The Cultural Politics of Markets: Economic Liberalization and Social Change in Nepal*. London: Pluto Press.

Regmi, M. 1977. *Landownership in Nepal.* New Delhi: Adroit Publishers.

Riaz, A. and S. Basu 2008. *Paradise Lost? Failure in Nepal.* Lanham, MD: Lexington Books.

Robertson, T.B. 2018. 'DDT and the Cold War Jungle: American Environmental and Social Engineering in the Rapti Valley of Nepal'. *Journal of American History*, 104(4): 904–930.

Roy, P. and M. Khan. 2017. *Nepal's Political Settlement and Inclusive Growth: Not Quite Business As Usual.* London: SOAS, University of London and ACE RPC.

Shah, S. 2008. *Civil Society in Uncivil Places: Soft State and Regime Change in Nepal*. Washington DC: East West Center.

Shah, S. 2018. *A Project of Memoriality: Transnational Development and Local Activism*. Kathmandu: Himal Books.

Sharma, J.R. 2008. 'Practices of Male Labor Migration from the Hills of Nepal to India in Development Discourses: Which Pathology?'. *Gender, Technology and Development*, 12(3): 303–323.

Sharma, J. and I. Harper. 2018 'Britain-Nepal Relations through the Prism of Aid'. *European Bulletin of Himalayan Research*, 50/51: 145–161.

Sharma, K., A. KC, M. Subedi, and B. Pokharel. 2018. 'Challenges for Reconstruction after *Mw*7.8 Gorkha Earthquake: A Study on a Devastated Area of Nepal'. *Geomatics, Natural Hazards and Risk*, 9 (1): 760–790.

Sharma, S. 2001. *Procuring Water: Foreign Aid and Rural Water Supply in Nepal*. Kathmandu: Nepal Water Conservation Foundation.

Shneiderman, S. and M. Turin. 2004. 'The Path to Janasarkar in Dolakha District: Towards an Ethnography of the Maoist Movement'. In *Himalayan People's War: Nepal's Maoist Rebellion*, edited by M. Hutt, 77–109. London: Hurst & Co.

Shrestha, R. Nanda. 1998. *In the Name of Development: A Reflection of Nepal*. Kathmandu: Educational Enterprises.

Skerry, C.A., K. Moran, and K.M. Calavan. 1991. *Four Decades of Development: The History of US Assistance to Nepal 1951–1991*. Kathmandu: USAID.

Stone, L. 1989. 'Cultural Crossroads of Community Participation in Development-A Case from Nepal'. *Human Organization*, 48: 206–213.

UN-OCHA. 2006. 'Nepal: Village Development Committee (VDC) Secretaries Displacement', as of July 2006. Available at: https://reliefweb.int/map/nepal/nepal-village-development-committee-vdc-secretaries-displacement-july-2006 (Accessed on 11 May 2021).

Tansen Palace, that housed several government offices, was attacked by the Maoist rebels on 31 January 2006.

6

Conclusion: Precarity and Paradox in Once-Remote Locations

It has become a cliché to talk about Nepal in terms of crisis and state failure. One of the earliest accounts of 'crisis' is found in Erik Eckholm's popular book, *Losing Ground* (1976), where he popularised the concept of environmental crisis in Nepal. He linked population growth to upland deforestation and soil erosion, which was causing widespread downstream flooding and silting. This became known as the 'Theory of Himalayan Environmental Degradation' (Guthman 2002). Similarly, Alan Macfarlane's authoritative book, *Resources and Population* (1976), based on fieldwork in a village north of Pokhara, argued that a massive environmental crisis was due as he predicted 'no forest by the year 2020'. Another very popular book titled *Nepal in Crisis* (1980) by Piers Blaikie, John Cameron and David Seddon, based on their research work in western-central Nepal in the 1970s, predicted a crisis and argued that the development of capitalism in Nepal is effectively precluded by Nepal's relationship with India, its class structures and the nature of the Nepali state (Blaikie et al. 1980). Similarly, on political developments, in their provocatively titled book, *Paradise Lost? State Failure in Nepal*, written in 2008, Ali Riaz and Subho Basu claimed that Nepali state had failed and located this failure in the history of the extractive patrimonial state in Nepal. Overwhelmed by the Maoist insurgency, severe human rights violations and looming humanitarian crisis, state failure discourses were prominent in the international policy discourses in the early and mid-2000s in Nepal. This is not an extensive survey of discourses on crisis, but these selected texts give an indication of how Nepal has been framed in terms of a crisis in need of external interventions.

While these authoritative accounts on crisis have led to the influx of aid into Nepal in the name of population control, family planning, environmental protection, agricultural development, governance, human rights, conflict management and peacebuilding, these foresights have not resulted in actual crisis or state failure. In other words, such discourses have remained imaginative and fictional. Furthermore, based on a restudy after 20 and 30 years, Blaikie and colleagues, and Macfarlane have revisited their earlier claims on crisis. In a more recent account, Macfarlane, reflecting on 30 years of change in the same Gurung village, points out that migration is possibly a major driving force behind the changes occurring in the studied village (Macfarlane 2001). The importance of remittance, as described in his original study, had declined to a thin trickle from the few labourers abroad, who saved a little and sent it home. His revisit showed that there was a change in the nature of migration. From the middle of the 1970s, when army recruitment dried up, people went first to India and later to East and South East Asia, the Middle East and a few to Europe and America. When they and the remaining army servicemen retired, they no longer came back to the village, but settled in the town, particularly in the nearby town of Pokhara. Further, he argued that the beneficial effect of this outmigration had been to prevent ecological collapse, but it has meant that the people left behind were bearing the burden of outmigration, visible in material impoverishment (Macfarlane 2001). Campbell has criticised Macfarlane's 'revised village history' for treating individuals as passive people who responded to changes as an overpowering fact of life. 'There seems to be a lack of fit between this component of reflexive engagement with the change, and the general undertow of the income-seeking migratory imperative' (Campbell 2001, 111). Similarly, Blaikie and colleagues went back to conduct a restudy after 20 years, where they conclude by saying 'the most important empirical conclusion about social change in rural western Nepal over 20 years is the degree of its continuity' (Blaikie et al. 2002, 1267). The restudy compared class structure over the 20 years and argued that there had been very little change in the rural class structure. In the restudy, however, the authors found that they had underestimated the importance of migration and urban growth in their original study and that these appear to have resulted in significant rural social change in Nepal, although they do indicate personal, social and economic tensions that could result from such dependence on outmigration.

Similarly, Nepal's political transition has been relatively peaceful. Despite contentious politics and protracted transition, a constitutional settlement was reached in 2015. Unlike what Riaz and Basu have argued, it would be difficult to find convincing evidence on state failure in Nepal. There is little doubt that Nepal has undergone a series of rapid political and economic changes, but framing such a transition as state failure is misguided, and shows the lack of a willingness to understand the historical process of state transformation. Thus, the framing as state failure completely ignores the process of intense political transition witnessed in Nepal in the last few decades. As indicated in Chapter One, not only has Nepal witnessed impressive political changes, but it has also seen significant improvements in its human development indicators and expansion of physical infrastructures, as well as an impressive increase in citizenship and rights. Further, post 2005, Nepal's 'political crisis' has been settled through a UN-mediated peace process and a radical restructuring of the Nepali state. The conservative framing of Nepal's political transition in terms of state failure obscures the impressive transition process witnessed in Nepal. Nepal has transitioned from a centralised, Hindu, monarchy to a federal, secular and republican state within a short period. As discussed earlier, there has been a tectonic shift in the nature of the Nepali state, where ideas of human rights and citizenship are now pervasive. This is seen in the various social and political movements demanding rights, recognition and redistribution of political and economic resources.

Although largely ignored by public and scholarly debate, Nepal has been going through a silent process of economic transformation from land- and agriculture-based livelihoods to non-land- and non-agriculture-based livelihoods alongside the country's incorporation in the global economy. The nature of land- and agrarian-based social relations have undergone significant changes, challenging historical inequalities based on land tenure and caste-based labour relations as remittance and other sources of cash have become new sources of power and income. The widespread increase in outmigration has had a significant impact on the subsistence agriculture and labour that sustained the moral economic institutions and norms. Nepali peasants who have been the subject of the extractive state have found new sources and hopes of economic and political freedom in far-flung emerging economies in the Gulf States and South East Asia, away from the land and agrarian relations that subjected them to poverty, inequality and exclusion. The rapid inflow of cash from remittance, which contributes to a third of the country's GDP, and the flow of other cash sources have significantly commodified rural life and altered social relations. The penetration of the market and varieties of market-induced financial infrastructures have commodified life in remote areas. The Nepali village today is no longer a self-contained closed economy and the dynamics of production and distribution have changed dramatically. It is no longer isolated from global financial markets. Remote rural villages have now become more closely integrated into the global capital.

Widespread labour mobility and remittance have brought new sources of freedom for labouring populations away from attached forms of caste-based labour and feudal relations. Such changes have profoundly impacted the loosening of the caste-based attached labour embedded in land-based livelihoods and social relations. Non-land-based livelihoods and mobility of labour have significant implications for feudal relations and caste. Widespread access to outmigration means that people no longer have to live within the proximity of upper-caste dominance on an everyday basis; although, this does not mean that the caste system has disappeared with outmigration. Caste-based attached labour has certainly declined, and so have caste-based rituals and observation of purity. The economic and political dominance of upper-caste men, however, has not declined. While upper-caste men continue to dominate public life, there are possibilities of that changing in the next decade with newly adopted affirmative action and increasing mobility patterns for higher education and employment.

Beyond economic implications, there are cultural consequences of this process. Labour migration is not just an economic process, but a sociocultural one. Remittance is not the only reason why Nepalis out-migrate. As I have argued elsewhere (Sharma 2019), migration has become a rite of passage and articulation of masculinity for young men in the face of economic uncertainty. There are sociocultural consequences of this process, as young people do not see their future in agriculture, and, instead, see migration as a source of escape and freedom from the regimented order of the village, although, in practice, it rarely results in freedom.

Despite these impressive political and economic changes and the end of the hereditary rule of the Ranas and Shahs, Nepal has seen the continuation of clientelisms and exclusion. Progressive political changes or modernising forces have not removed deep-rooted patronage-based power and politics. Paradoxically, patronage systems have continued and thrived under the guises of democracy. New sources of vulnerabilities have emanated from collusive practices, as businesses, politicians and bureaucrats collude, that are hidden under the democratic fabric. Reflecting on the reality of wider South Asia, people turn out to vote in large numbers and actively take part in public debates, criticising the state and politicians, despite knowing they cannot make political leaders accountable. Democracy exists, but poor people hardly have access to politicians between elections. It is common practice that people exchange votes for material goods or at least view it that way. People view politicians as agents who distribute material goods or who facilitate access to basic services. Accordingly, this is reflected in the lobbying by local and - national - level politicians for more resources (such as various avatars of the 'Member of Parliament Development Fund'), which they can spend in their constituencies and sustain their patronage networks. In such a context, development strategies will need to acknowledge the real politics of patronage, rather than making attempts to get rid of it as a 'traditional practice'. Patronage practices, such as *aafno manche* or *chakari*, are not just rooted in a caste-based culture; these are also local idioms of distribution and social networks.

Unlike the fear of overpopulation prominent in the 1970s, causing an agrarian crisis, food insecurity, environmental degradation and poverty, Nepal has witnessed very rapid demographic changes in the last few decades as a result of the transition from a high-mortality, high-fertility society to a low mortality, a low-fertility society within a relatively short period. This demographic transition has changed the age structure of Nepal's population, resulting in a 'bulge' in the working age group. In theory, this demographic shift offers a window of opportunity. The increased share in the working age population is seen as a 'demographic dividend' with economic development potential. However, sluggish job creation has meant that Nepal's demographic dividend is being missed. Instead, Nepal has adopted the policy of encouraging outmigration of its working age population, thus, outsourcing the benefits of the demographic dividend to labour-receiving countries in the Gulf States, South East Asia and India among others. Thus, Nepal's demographic dividend does not seem to benefit Nepal, although it has certainly played an important role in keeping poverty rates low, paying for health and education and feeding the dependent population albeit at a high cost.

This transfer of the demographic dividend as overseas labour migration has significant costs. First, the system of migrant labour that separates the production of labour from production from labour (Burawoy 1976) means that it is the destination economies that benefit from the surplus population from remote rural areas of Nepal, in addition to the economic and political elite who benefit from the rent produced by the migration and remittance industry. Second, Nepali migrants are subjected to widespread exploitation, illtreatment, injury and death during transit, and while working in the destination. Third, while the Nepali elite benefit from remittance transfer that covers a third of Nepal's GDP and also the economic and political elite who benefit from the economic values (from recruitment, foreign exchange and consumption), outmigration has a detrimental impact on those left behind. As migrant workers travel to produce and benefit the destination economies, the caring and reproduction are done by those left behind. Furthermore, those left behind must care for the diseased, injured and old migrant workers. Migrant workers can work, earn and remit only because those left behind look after the household and offer insurance at the time of old age, illness and eventual retirement, when the migrant body becomes redundant, having exhausted their usefulness in a precarious economy overseas. Thus, the migrants and their left-behind households are subjected to multiple layers of exploitation.

Moreover, Nepal's demographic transition also comes with a challenge, that is, a rapidly growing 'ageing society', one where the percentage of people aged between 65 years and above (so-called 'old-age dependants') accounts for 7 per cent or more of the total population. If this value doubles to 14 per cent, the society is then considered 'aged'. According to a calculation by the Population Council, Nepal will become an 'ageing society' around 2028, and an aged society around 2054 (NPC and UNICEF 2017). Such rapid transitions to ageing and aged societies mean it will not be easy for the working age population to migrate overseas for work, leaving those in need of care behind.

Even if jobs are available in global destinations, difficult choices will need to be made on caring for the elderly back in the village.

Migrant labour and remittance have emerged as massive sources of freedom and opportunities and contributed to a decline in poverty and improvement in human development indicators. However, they have simultaneously exposed households to new sources of uncertainties and precarity, whereby, they have very little control over their lives. There is, what I have called a development paradox, that is, despite notable changes in several development indicators, there are new vulnerabilities, risks and precarity associated with dependence on labour migration. The recent coronavirus pandemic of 2019 has exposed and made visible the plight and precarity of Nepali migrant workers in overseas destinations. While it was natural for migrant workers to attempt to return home at the time of uncertainty, many were left stranded at the Indo–Nepal border or in the migration destinations as they attempted to return or lost their jobs. Others, eager to leave Nepal as migrant workers, found themselves trapped in political, economic and public health forces beyond their comprehension and control.

All these factors show that Nepal has undergone a significant process of social transformation. However, what are the possibilities for the 'Great Transformation' in Nepal in the Polanyian sense? As I have argued in this book, to put it simply, there has been a massive transformation in Nepal in the domains of politics, society and economy, yet it is unlikely that Nepal will see a 'Great Transformation' in a Polanyian sense. To borrow from Nancy Fraser, while transformation in Nepal appears to follow Polanyian structural logic, it does not seem to follow the political logic of double movement put forward by Polanyi (Fraser 2013).

Polanyi's concept of *double movement* offers a useful framework to understand both how the economy is embedded in society and its transformation to a disembedded economy. There is clear evidence of Nepal witnessing the elements of the first movement from a pre-market and pre-industrial system to what Polanyi called market society, although this transformation is not a linear one, but a simultaneous one. This transformation is most widely visible in the commodification of labour, land and widespread use of money in rural Nepal. Labour in rural areas has become commodified; old systems of reciprocal labour exchange and attached labour have been largely replaced by wage labour, although they haven't been completely wiped out. Money has become widely available, significantly disrupting the moral economic institutions and norms. While the use of cash has been prompted by the land and taxation policy of the Nepali state prompting distressed outmigration, its use has become widespread only in the recent decades with widespread penetration of roads, consumer goods, financial products and widespread circulation of remittances. As road networks penetrate remote rural areas, the land has become commodified with significant repercussions for agriculture and environment. While land continues to be associated with belonging and lineage, cities and towns have seen significant commodification of land, as real estate agents and brokers continue to divide the land into small plots leading to speculative price rise.

While the market liberalism took its strongest shape in Nepal in the 1980s, the commodification of land, labour and money began much earlier. In the context of Nepal, critical political economic processes have included the recruitment of Nepali men in the British Army, extractive land and taxation policies. These precede the market liberalism of 1980s and 1990s. The recruitment of Nepali men in the British Army introduced the widespread use of cash in rural economy. Similarly, the land reform and taxation policy of the state not only promoted private ownership of land, but also required peasants to pay their tax in cash, prompting peasants to sell their produce in the market to generate cash.

The commodification of land and labour with lack of regulation and protection has brought new sources of conflict, loss and anxieties.

These processes have brought significant disruption in the moral economy, impacting the social, economic and environmental fabric of life. So, despite the disruptive impact of the market, why haven't we seen a countermovement from below in Nepal?

Nepal's democratisation provides an optimistic environment for countermovement, particularly since the numerical majority have below-average incomes, and are disproportionately lacking in social protection. The year 1990 saw a major political change in Nepal where the absolute monarchy was replaced by a multiparty democracy. The new constitution gave rise to extensive political and social rights in Nepal, in addition to the expansion of Nepal's public sphere—media, professional organisations, ethnic organisations and NGOs. Trade unions came to be visible in the public sphere albeit as loyal cadres of political parties who have not been seen raising the concerns of the labouring populations. There was the abolishment of bonded labour although newly freed labour was left without any protection, who were, thus, forced to work under exploitative conditions in the unregulated market. The 1990s did not see a countermovement, from any section of society, including intellectuals, on the question of livelihoods or the protection of the most vulnerable from the ill effects of markets. As discussed earlier, the notable movements from below were based on ethnic, linguistic and regional identities and aimed at greater recognition, rights and representation. Even the Maoist insurgency, which started as a class-based peasant movement, quickly abandoned the question of class, peasantry or livelihoods.

The characteristics of major social and political movements that emerged in Nepal since the 1990s are qualitatively different than Polanyian countermovement calling for social protection. The social and political movements witnessed in Nepal have called for multiculturalism, recognition and democratisation whose aims have not been to protect society from the whims of the market forces, but to free it from domination that have historically emanated from within society in the form of religion, caste, ethnicity, language and gender.

Thus, Nepal's case shows that while there has been impressive social and political movements from below, demanding identity, recognition, rights and citizenship, these countermovements have largely refrained from asking critical questions on the importance of caste, ethnicity and gender as a structure of advantage and discrimination in the modern political-economic systems and the questions of harms emanating from deregulation of market and economic forces. Nepal's impressive social and political movements have been preoccupied with the idea of 'social inclusion' and 'state-restructuring' rooted in a particular reading of Nepal's nationalist history. The countermovement in Nepal have largely been discursive and focussed on the recognition of identity and distribution of power from the state in the form of state-restructuring, rights and citizenship and affirmative action that have yet to articulate the questions of life and livelihoods of the most vulnerable. There is no noticeable resistance to widespread commodification of money, land and labour associated with market deregulation. Gender, caste or ethnicity are not just old forms of cultural domination to be remedied through reservation policies in government jobs but are also embedded in modern labour market and market economy. There is no state-sponsored social protection system or prospect of minimum income guarantee in Nepal. There is piecemeal social protection from the state in the form of old age allowance and window allowance, which are negligent with very low payments and limited reach, and there is no middle class or working class or civil society or intellectual class political force calling for social protection.

The middle classes or civil society movements in Nepal haven't raised the issue of economic precarity or precarious lives in Nepal that are rooted in the ideas and policies of deregulation. There have not been organised attempts by the state or the civil society groups to protect the poor and marginalised in Nepal from the whims of market forces, whether at home or overseas. Unlike in developed countries, where the impact of market liberalisation on livelihoods was cushioned by social security systems and the market was managed with extensive regulation, in Nepal, social security or the regulatory system has been limited or non-existent. It is only in the new millennium that intermittent discussion on social security and protection has begun to enter the development policy vocabulary through donor-funded piecemeal projects in Nepal. Likewise, the introduction of the market in organisation of labour or the entry of real estate agents and agencies in land transaction is not completely isolated from political and social influences.

The nature of precarity in Nepal has strong roots in global labour migration and broader processes of circulation of cash and financialisation. The Nepali state has pursued a simultaneous policy of encouraging labour outmigration and the protection of Nepali migrants overseas. One of the key events was the commodification of labour for the overseas market that started with the exporting of Nepal's labour through Nepal's Foreign Employment Act (1985). In the context of Nepal, the promotion of overseas labour migration[1] demands a closer analysis of the commodification, exploitation, protection and rights of this group of the population, not just within the history of Nepal, but also as a part of the global capital. In overseas labour migration, only limited reform has begun with concerns on the appalling condition of migrant workers in various destinations.

Unlike in Europe, a very different history of capitalist development has largely prevented the development of the social protection system in the first place. While countries like India or South Africa are seeing some form of distributive politics in the form of large-scale social protection programmes via cash transfer, we are unlikely to see such development of this in Nepal. The 'movement from below', as Polanyi would like us to believe, has been occupied with identity-based movements and there has not been any indication of class-based

1 Until 2018, Nepal's Foreign Employment Board was called Foreign Employment Promotions Board.

movement or a broad-based movement calling for protection from the disruptive impact of the market and precarities that emanate from the process of overseas labour migration or destructive development activities. The discussion on enforcement of minimum wage, protection of labouring population, including migrant workers, who are consistently ill-treated and exploited, has not featured prominently in the public or political debate. The limited raising of issues by NGOs, media and civil society has not resulted in the articulation of people's vulnerability in the face of joblessness, precarity and exploitative overseas labour. The transnational nature of the market forces in contemporary Nepal means that the social movements and social policy will need to address the harms emanating from overseas labour migration. Small-scale welfare interventions of NGOs and CBOs are unlikely to offer social protection for many. The Maoist insurgency and the subsequent Comprehensive Peace Agreement is a good example of how a radical movement from below that started as a peasant/class movement graduated to abandon all the pertinent questions when it came to the UN-led peace process. In the absence of any social protection from the state or other actors, people have relied on their kinship-based social and political networks to deal with vulnerabilities and increasingly precarious situations they find themselves in. In the context of precarious employment and life, its cost is borne not just by the individual migrants or the migrant households, but also by the extended family and kinship networks.

References

Blaikie, P., J. Cameron, and D. Seddon. 1980. *Nepal in Crisis: Growth and Stagnation at the Periphery.* Delhi, Oxford University Press.

Blaikie, P., J. Cameron, and D. Seddon. 2002. 'Understanding 20 Years of Change in West-Central Nepal: Continuity and Change in Lives and Ideas'. *World Development*, 30: 1255–1270.

Campbell, B. 2001. 'Locating Population and Resources'. *European Bulletin for Himalayan Research*, 20 (1): 110–12.

Eckholm, E. 1976. *Losing Ground: Environmental Stress and World Food Prospects*. New York: W.W. Norton.

Macfarlane, A. 1976. *Resources and Population: A Study of Gurungs of Nepal.* London: Cambridge University Press.

Macfarlane, A. 2001. 'Sliding Downhill: Some Reflections on Thirty years of Change in a Himalayan Village'. *European Bulletin for Himalayan Research*, 20: 105–110.

Riaz, A. and Basu, S. 2008. *Paradise Lost? Failure in Nepal.* Lanham, MD: Lexington Books.

Sharma, J.R. 2019. *Crossing the Border to India: Youth, Migration and Masculinities in Nepal.* New Delhi: Bloomsbury.

Index

D

E

F

G

About the Author

Jeevan R. Sharma is a Senior Lecturer in South Asia and International Development at the University of Edinburgh. He is the author of *Crossing the Border to India: Youth, Migration and Masculinities in Nepal*, Temple University Press, 2018 (South Asian Edition published by Bloomsbury Academic India in 2019). He has carried out anthropological research on culture of migration, politics of aid-funded interventions in Nepal and on low-income migrants in Indian cities. His work has focussed on labour migration in the context of social, economic and political transformations in Nepal, the Himalayas and the South Asian region, especially the culture of migration; border crossing; gendered, classed and racialised mobility of labour; ill treatment; access to justice and citizenship in South Asia. He is the co-editor of *Himalaya* and an associate editor of *South Asia: Journal of South Asian Studies*.